A LIFETIME OF PREPARATION

By Steve Gant

Thank you for being a
Here 2 there Partner!

Grace + peace,

Psalm 1:1-3

PRAISE FOR THE BOOK

"This is the walk through the gritty reality of decades of missed moments, poor choices, and a closed heart, yet reminds us that God is still at work and powerful enough to soften a heart and reawaken a relationship with Him through Christ.

It is a fresh reminder of the dangers of regret is always asking, "What if I had only listened sooner or chosen differently?" The better course and the challenge found in the pages of "A Lifetime of Preparation," is to start serving God now where He has planted or where He directs."

- James Grunwald
2-Time Olympian
(Wrestling)

"Steve's life story is a tremendous encouragement for us all, and for men in particular. We men typically do not connect our life experiences and choices as being a divinely orchestrated spiritual journey designed to become the unique ministry calling, we were each built for. Steve's story is an inspiration for each of us to seek *our ministry calling*, revealed by God *through our story!"*

-Bob Graumann
Iron Sharpens Iron, Field Rep

"From a true sailor's life, to the mission field of Africa, Stephen Gant will take you on a journey only God could direct. Like a lot of men, Stephen had to hit rock bottom where he cried out to God! God answered in a mighty way. God sent Stephen and his wife into the African prisons where they had a successful ministry. God used that and moved them throughout the country ministering to families and children in Jesus' name. Stephen now sees how God had prepared him throughout his entire life for this mission. As you read, ask God what is the mission He has prepared you for."

-    **Paul Lee**
Executive Director
Fellowship of Christian Peace Officers-USA

This book is a guaranteed best seller!

-    **Carol Gant**
(Mom)

WHAT READERS ARE SAYING:

"An excellent example of how God can take the broken tile of someone's life and make a beautiful mosaic masterpiece. "

"This man's story could be every man's story."

"A remarkable journey from darkness to Light."

"Gant's honesty and humility invites us into failures, heartaches and a transformation through Christ."

"This is by far my favorite book I have ever read! I have never read a humbler yet real memoir ever!"

"A story of moving from a self-focused, self-motivated, hard-working American success story to a sold-out, Christ-centered, others-focused follower of Jesus Christ. I enjoyed reading about his life's transformation and was motivated to do some self-examination of my own walk with Christ."

DEDICATION

Firstly, I want to dedicate this book to my Lord and Savior Jesus Christ who died on the cross for my sins to save me. If you get anything from this book, I hope it is how much He loves us.

Secondly, I want to dedicate this book to the ladies of my life. To the love of my life, my wife Gina. Your love and support through our years of marriage have afforded me the opportunity to pursue the things God has placed before me. You do things behind the scenes that no one will ever see, but without them I could not survive. You have always relished the opportunity to serve those around you, which sounds easy to the common person, but I now understand that it is one of the highest forms of sacrificial love. You find it so easy to put others first.

I admire the counsel that you give to so many, including myself. Your phone never seems to stop ringing—whether it is a friend who needs advice or just a sympathetic ear to listen, you are there. You assume the heartbreaking role of being a foster mom to so many children that need a home and stability. You continue answering calls and sitting in court with moms in danger of losing their parental rights, taking the time to counsel them and lovingly explain the system. What amazes me the most is your willingness to be that friend, always asking the question, "How are you?"

Thank you to my daughters, Ashton, and Gabrielle, for always being my encouragement and my purpose. I am incredibly proud of the ladies you have become, and you have given me two sons-in-law I can be equally proud of. Thank you for your grace and mercy when I fall short, and for teaching me the lessons I needed to learn about being a dad. Always remember to set your goals high and your eyes on the Lord. One of the things that motivates me the most in life is the example I set for my Lord and you girls. I pray for you and your husbands every day. I want my grandchildren to remember their Granddaddy as a man who loves his family, the Lord and worked hard to tell others about the love of Jesus. My life is truly better with you in it, and I can think of no higher honor in this world then being your dad. I am always here for you and am your biggest fan. XOXO.

FOREWORD

Occasionally you run across a person that impresses you from the very first time you meet them. Stephen Gant is one of those individuals. In my fourteen years leading the Student Life department at Trinity Baptist College, I have crossed paths with many students. I can still remember the first time I met Stephen, and this is based on more than the fact that he was attending freshman orientation as a forty-something! It was evident to me from the start that Stephen was a gifted leader. He spoke with confidence, and both students and college faculty responded well to his genuine care and concern for them as individuals. Most adult learners choose not to engage deeply with the campus community. They attend classes and then immerse themselves in the busyness of their own lives. This is understandable for many reasons, but it is this break from what is typical that makes Stephen Gant stand out plainly. During his time at TBC, Stephen intentionally invested countless hours into the community of TBC. His classmates even voted him in as Student Body

Chaplain his senior year, a position that is rarely ever held by an adult learner at our institution.

Over the course of four years, I began to get to know Stephen on a personal level and was amazed by his dedication and commitment to live his life in service to the Great Commission. In my conversation with Stephen, he was always talking about his current efforts to make disciples of Jesus Christ and his future plans to continue doing this kingdom work, both domestically and abroad. I enjoyed hearing the stories of his many life adventures and seeing first-hand how God had been preparing Stephen over the course of his entire life to do amazing things for the advancement of the gospel, especially overseas. The stories from his time in the Navy were especially riveting. I am so glad that Stephen has chosen to write these stories down so that they can be enjoyed by the readers of this book. Stephen has challenged my own ideas of what leadership looks like. He leads from the front, but at the same time has a genuine care and concern for those around him.

I remember on one specific occasion going to Stephen's house to visit him, along with our mutual friend, Vaughn Brown, when Stephen was recovering from breaking his foot on a mission's trip to Guyana. My goal was to be an encouragement to Stephen, but after experiencing his genuine hospitality, I remember leaving

Stephen's house thinking that I was the one that had been encouraged.

Stephen and his wife Gina both live out the gospel story in their lives. They have opened their home on many occasions to strangers and those in need. This is especially exemplified in their work with foster children. I am reminded of the words of Jesus when he said, "Whoever welcomes one of these little children in my name welcomes me..." These words epitomize the life of Stephen Gant. I am confident that anyone reading this book will be inspired to give and serve more. Reading these words and seeing them lived out in Stephen's life have also inspired me deeply.

During my time at Trinity Baptist College, I have known many students that have passed through our campus, many of whom have gone on to do incredible things for the sake of God's kingdom. Stephen's story is unique to most of them in the fact that Stephen came to college already prepared to do ministry. The heartbeat of ministry is people, and during his time at Trinity Stephen sacrificially gave of his time to invest in so many. Stephen will tell you that he attended TBC in order to better prepare himself to do ministry work. I would argue that eternity might reveal that his time at TBC was one of his greatest ministry moments. The countless students that he encouraged, befriended, mentored, discipled, and led will be one of Stephen's most lasting legacies. It is evident to me that God had used a lifetime of preparation to position Stephen perfectly for this fruitful season of ministry.

Many people have taken the time to write their life story, but few stories have more evidence of God's sovereign care and guidance than Stephen's. After reading this book I am sure that you will agree with me that no one can bring a series of life events together in a greater way than God can! What makes Stephen's story so captivating is the fact that God is so clearly at work throughout each chapter of Stephen's life.

I am honored to have been asked to write the foreword to this book and wholeheartedly believe that God's hand is upon Stephen's life. I am looking forward to seeing what the "next" chapter in his life holds, and "I am confident that he who began a good work in him will bring it to completion at the day of Jesus Christ."

Dr. Jeremiah Stanley

Vice President of Student Affairs
Trinity Baptist College
Jacksonville, FL

A
Lifetime
of
Preparation

INTRODUCTION

WARNING: If you're looking for a feel good, fluffy-kittens, unicorns, and rainbows kind of mission's book, this is not it. This is the story of one man's walk of death on the wide road that would leave behind countless causalities, who found the narrow road using God's word. This then resulted in my spiritual rebirth, and after some time in the wilderness, and trial by fire, I could finally walk in life.

This testimony is a journey deep inside my personal world. A journey that took me from my small southern roots in SC, to the world of global missions and beyond. A journey that reminds us of the challenges of the countless crossroads that each person will face in life where there are two paths to choose from, and the devil is there to disrupt us every time.

This book is a journey of self-discovery that was written during one of those crossroad decisions. It made me push myself further than I wanted to go, removed the scales from my eyes, and allowed me to see as clear as I had ever seen before.

I have always wanted to write a book but was never sure of the topic. I have made a few attempts at it, but nothing really stuck. I did not think I could ever get myself to sit down long enough to get anything on paper. As I sit here in my study, looking out the window over the African countryside, I take stock of what brought me here today and how a young girl helped me unlock the truth of myself.

My cousin Kim has four children, and their lives are a testimony to all who observe them. As a single mom on one income, she has raised four loving children any parent would be proud of. In 2014, during our first year in Africa as missionaries, my wife Gina and I received an email from Kim's oldest daughter, Cori, with two requests. The first was that she was doing a project for school, and she had to interview a missionary. Her second request was that we mention God as much as we could in the answers. Well, I did not want to let her down on that one. So, I sat down feeling much like Earnest Hemingway, ready to weave the masterpiece that would be my opus.

THE EMAIL:

Hey! It's Cori, thank you so much for taking the time to do this. So, I only have 10 quick questions for you.

#1 What makes someone qualified to be a missionary?

BOOM! I was stumped on the very first question. Qualified? Is there a qualification? I had been a lot of things in life, a welder, metal worker, and firefighter. I had spent time in the classroom as an instructor, facilitator and had become a chemical/biological weapons defense expert. But Missionary? No. Not one class in my twelve years of public education or twenty years of naval service had prepared me for this moment. Or had it? Throughout these life events, I have seen many things, experienced crushing heartache, and lived through the lowest of lows. I have witnessed life's highs with the births of my children and at times seemed to be surrounded by death, like I was sharing a gym locker with the Grim Reaper himself.

So, when Cori presented this question to me in her interview, I accepted the challenge and did what any military man would do; I started to make a list. I began to look over my past and list the events and experiences that could have prepared me to be a missionary. I looked at my own history and my walk with the Lord, and I knew that I always tried to do the best I could, but it was never enough. The road of life can be narrow, rocky, and full of twists and turns. The narrow path is less worn because it is less traveled. The road of life can be rocky and filled with obstacles that can trip us up. It also has many forks where we must make decisions. The guard rails of God's Word keeps us on the narrow path if we choose to heed it. We learn from our stumbles; we grow in the wisdom and the decisions that God helps us to make. Pray today for God to make your path straight and for His wisdom in your journey.

There was a very popular bumper sticker back in the day. "God is my Co-pilot." I found that to be bad advice. That would mean that I steer my life and ask for God's assistance just when I get off track. Ask yourself if God is your co-pilot in life or, is He the Pilot? Throughout life, I know that God never left me or forsook me. Whether I was trying to be a rock musician, construction worker, or US Navy chief petty officer. Whether it was a missionary in Uganda, a father of two, or father of many children all over the world. My prayer is that this book provides some insight into the wide road of a sinful life, the glory of reconciliation to the Father, and the world of the missionary living in a foreign land.

My focus is to follow Revelation 12:11: *"And they overcame him by the blood of the Lamb, and by the word of their testimony; and they loved not their lives unto the death."*

Washed in the blood of the lamb, my focus is to get my testimony down on paper. Now that I can see clearly, I understand through the blessings, short-comings and learning opportunities, God is there, I just had to step up and step out. As a believer, it is never too late to get some skin in the game.

My wife Gina and I are regular people who felt God's calling on us. No matter how far you may think you are off track in life, God can make you new in Him, washed in His blood, bathed in His Grace. What will you do for Him?

God has taken me on a step-by-step journey to understand the plan He has for my life. I did not always understand God's plan for me, or even see the connections each life event had, but they have been there. As I get older, I now see that God's hand was all around me. Sometimes we become so desensitized, we miss what is going on right in front of our eyes. I now understand that with every high and low, every twist and turn, He is with me.

When I look back on every friendship I made, every pinnacle I reached, every low point I hit, life was filled with opportunities, and no time was wasted time. God gives us what we need to apply that we have learned in the past for Him. My hope is that this story resonates with you, and that you realize it is never too late to get right with the Lord. Now that I am truly saved, I walk in faith, and my life is very different, I do not look back on those times as wasted years, but as a part of my lifetime of preparation.

Chapter 1

IN THE BEGINNING, GOD CREATED... OPPORTUNITY

"Man got into difficulty when he lifted his will against God's. He gets out of trouble when he bows to the divine superiority, when he repents and says humbly: 'God be merciful to me a sinner. Man's extremity then becomes God's opportunity."

- **Billy Graham**

AS MY TWENTY YEARS in the US Navy was coming to a close, I had six months left in my career. The last ship I was stationed on was the USS *Samuel B. Roberts* FFG 58, and I had just returned from our third deployment in Western Africa. We had many tasks assigned while floating six months off the coast: anti-drug operations, pulling over illegal fishing vessels, and combating human trafficking. All these things had one thing in common; fighting criminals who were making money to support terrorism worldwide. Every once in a while, we would pull into a port for some rest and relaxation which would normally include a night of drinking and hanging out in some seedy club run by dangerous men.

While we were in port, we would sometimes be asked to conduct some community relations projects or, as we called them, COMREL. Because I was a good leader and organizer, I was chosen to be the Community Relations Representative for the command. I was assigned to work alongside the ship's chaplain, Chaplain Murphy. Chaplain Murphy was a young officer but had loads of scriptural wisdom. He would always make time to counsel the men even if it was over a beer at the bar or a cigar in the smoking area onboard. He was one of the guys, and he meet everyone right where they were.

When we'd pull into port, Chaplain Murphy and I would be picked up by a local driver and would visit a school, hospital, or orphanage that needed our help. The government officials would tell us the needs of the people and I'd take notes and plan for the project material and manpower required for the job.

On one tour, we went to a medical facility in Lagos, Nigeria. We were tasked to install 150 hanging mosquito nets for 150 cribs in what seemed like a large warehouse. The windows of the warehouse had no glass or screen, so the children were always susceptible to mosquitos and malaria. Although the lack of glass did bring a breeze, it did not do much to disperse the smell.

While dressed in my finest pressed Khakis and ribbons, ready to pose for pictures, I was quickly handed one of the babies from one of the cribs to hold. The local news people snapped pictures, and we exchanged small talk with the caretakers.

Using a French translator, I asked the nurse, "Are all these children orphans?"

Shaking her head, she responded in her best broken English, "No, they are not all orphans."

Relieved I replied, "Oh well that's good."

The nurse then touched my arm to get my attention. "Some of them do have parents, but all of these children have HIV, and so do the parents who live."

As I scanned the room and saw crib after crib after crib, I felt a sense of dread and despair come over me. For the first time, a chink in my man armor appeared. I was one of the tough ones, but at that moment, I started to tear up. I was afraid I was going to cry, and I believe the nurse saw it and patted me on the shoulder as if to comfort me. A tear fell on my uniform, and the cameras started going off.

Driving back from that visit, I could feel that there was something bigger I could be doing, but what was it? The Navy was my life, and everything I knew. I loved being a Chief, and I loved the brotherhood of the Chief's Mess. I loved being a leader, a mentor. The Navy was who I was. I could always depend on the Navy because it would never let me down.

Throughout our lives, we are presented with opportunities that will shape us and our character. Events and life choices will come into our lives that will define who we are forever. Lagos, Nigeria was one of those moments.

GROWING UP IN THE SOUTH

I was born in Charleston, SC, not far away from the city of Sumter, and my parents adopted me when I was less than a year old. People ask me what it's like to be adopted. To be honest with you, I have no idea at all. From as early as I could remember, I had always known I was adopted.

My parents picked me up from Columbia, SC, Sep 15th, 1971, when I was five months old. The law stated that it would not be a legal adoption until the one-year anniversary, so one year to the day the papers were signed, and I became their son. During that one-year trial adoption period, they found out my soon-to-be mom was pregnant with my brother. On Sep 15th, 1972, the papers were signed, and two days later, my brother David was born.

Every year on April 30th, we would celebrate my birthday like every other child's. We would have a party, gifts, cake, friends etc. But on Sep 15th, my adoption day, I would get a pie that read "Joy Boy." What kid wouldn't want two parties a year? It was not a big event like a birthday party, but it was made special for me. It reminded me of reading Mark Twain's book, where Tom Sawyer tricks Ben into whitewashing the fence. "Boy, it sure is fun whitewashing this fence." Not to say they tricked me into it, but it is all about perspective. They had made something that could have been viewed as negative and made it positive, so as I grew up, I was always aware of it. In fact, to me it was normal. They chose to tell me early, made it a celebration, and never tried to hide it. Adoption is a gift from God, an opportunity to give a child a loving home, with a loving family. I could not imagine a life without my adoptive parents.

My father, Robert M. Gant Jr, was by calling a pastor at Frasier Memorial Presbyterian church in Sumter, SC. This is the church where I would spend most of my childhood and be introduced to the Word of God. As a child, I loved the Good News Bible because it had stick figure pictures in it, and they were fun to look at.

I always tried to be a good son, but I was not always the best student; in fact, I was awful at it. Math was never my thing, but I did love Science and working with my hands. My friends and I would build tree houses and contraptions in our back yard on Curtiswood that resembled my favorite shows at the time *The Little Rascals* and *Gilligan's Island*.

Reflecting on some of the things we built, I am surprised we survived. At one point, we had built a three-story tree house made from trash and scrap wood found by the roadside. It had a crow's nest that was twenty-five feet off the ground, held up by only four rusty nails. Somehow the laws of gravity did not exist in our backyard, and I can now trace this back to an early proof that God was watching over me. We never bought any building supplies; all materials came from digging in the neighborhood trash. We used to drag home some of the worst stuff, and the corner of our back yard started to look like an episode from Sanford and Son.

The three-level house had many different rooms: a bathroom, living room, and reading room complete with a stack of Playboy magazine's we had brought from someone's garbage. The second floor had a fireplace—yes, a fireplace in a wooden tree house. I put bricks in a square and placed dirt on top of the wood floor to transfer some of the heat away from the wood, I told you I loved science.

Those Saturday morning shows whether it was The Adventures of *Gilligan's Island* and my first love Mary Ann or the inventions the professor would make to try get them off the island, television was a learning experience. The shows like *The Little Rascals* and Bob Villas, and *This Old House* would influence me greatly throughout my life. At that time, Saturday morning was the only time for kids shows.

I am sure my parents worried about what we were getting into, but they never stifled our creative flow, whether it was our questionable tree-house-construction practices or how my brother David and I would practice the comedic genius of *The Three Stooges*, complete with face slapping, and eye poking. I am sometimes shocked that we survived with all our fingers and eyes intact.

Mom and Dad never seemed to worry about us at all, so it seemed. I remember riding my bike to school on my own when I was in 4th grade. We would be gone the entire day, riding bikes, running in the woods, and hanging out under the bridge by the railroad tracks.

One time, my best friend and I were hanging out under a bridge. We made a small fire, put some pine straw down for beds, and started cooking a can of beans. Shortly after we started to cook our beans, a police officer came down under the bridge to see where the smoke was coming from. He began to survey the situation and asked what we thought we were doing. I began to explain to him in my best reasoning voice that it was all under control, and we were hobos trying to get by. He just laughed, kicked dirt on the fire, and told us to get lost. I think back on that now and wonder why he never even asked who we were, where we were from, or where we even got the matches. I guess those were different times altogether.

Sunday services, Wednesday night prayer meetings, and the rare Friday night special programs, like missionary visits were the main focal point of my family. Out of all of them, the missionary visits were my favorite. The missionaries would talk about the work they were doing and bring some things for us to look at from their field, like jewelry, baskets, or a snakeskin.

I had always known who Jesus was. I had always heard His name, so I always just knew. Just like when I was adopted, I just knew. One of my earliest memories in the church was as a small boy. During the statement of faith, we would mention Jesus was "delivered unto Pontius Pilate" to be crucified, and I remember thinking they were saying "unconscious pilot". Was Jesus also in World War II with Granddaddy Gant? Why was he unconscious? I look back and laugh at that now every time I hear it.

Growing up in the church had its advantages and disadvantages. Frasier Memorial Presbyterian Church was a small southern church of about fifty to sixty members, mostly made up of seven families that all were branched off from each other. It was a very tight group, and those days in the church were some of the best days of my life. It was all about fellowship. Church potlucks with sweet tea, fried chicken, potato salad, and Mrs. Dinky's special cake, which could cause a riot if there wasn't enough. My friend David Geddings and I would see who could eat the most fried chicken or shoot hoops in the parking lot between church and Sunday School.

Our youth group was made up of six people, three of whom were myself, my older sister, Robin, and my younger brother, David. Tommy Timmons was our youth group leader and one of the coolest guys we knew. He was a TV repair man back in the days when you still fixed TV's. He was a great influence on us and was placed into our lives at the right time.

Tommy owned a lot of pigeons and entered them in the Sumter County Fair every year. One day, he got me a job at the fair, taking blood samples for the chickens and livestock to prevent contamination of the other animals. He let my brother David and I pick one of his pigeons that we thought would win a prize at the fair. When the judging was over, out of all the birds at the fair, two of his had won first and second place. And both winners were the ones we had picked! Now either we were the best pigeon judges around, or we were just lucky. I believe we were lucky, and not for picking the right birds, but for having a friend and mentor like Tommy.

My lesson from Tommy was to do something good for someone, even when no one was watching. He taught me about sacrificing for others just for the sake of friendship. He would drive us kids all the way to the Carowinds theme park on the NC/SC border so we could ride all the rides. He would take us around and watch us get on the rides and come off and ask us how it was, but he himself would never ride them. He told me too much movement made him sick, so he was just there to let us have fun.

Another time, my favorite band, Van Halen, was playing at the Carolina Coliseum in Columbia, SC, and I wanted to get tickets to attend. Now this was long before the internet, so you were forced to leave your house and stand in line for tickets at a ticket office. To get the best tickets, or tickets at all, you had to get in line early. Tommy not only talked my dad into letting us go to the Van Halen concert, but he agreed to sleep outside on the sidewalk in front of the Seaco Music ticket office all night with us, so we could get the best seats. We set up chairs and stayed up all night, sitting on the sidewalk with blankets. The next day, we were first in line when they opened, and we got front-row tickets.

Tommy had no children and was like an uncle to us. He taught me the value of friendship and sacrifice for others. He was a humble man to the core and never bragged about anything, except how fast his Monte Carlo would go.

Going to those concerts my love for music began to grow. When it comes to music, I had tried a few things. I played clarinet in middle school. Which really was not the coolest instrument for a young boy, but it was fun at that time. Music was not the reason I joined the school band; it was because of a girl named

Kristen Cardarelli. Kristen played trumpet, and I sat directly across from her in the clarinet section. It was fun for a while, then grades started to come out, and I was quickly moved into a different direction, and I never even built up the nerve to speak to her.

I had to go home and tell my dad that I was failing at band and needed to drop out of the class. It was not like I set out to fail, I was just doing it for the wrong reason, which was a girl. No one starts out in life with a plan to fail, to wake up one morning saying, "Today I will strive for mediocracy." Our nature is to set goals and set them high, to reach for the dream of who we are meant to be. Our parents are there to encourage that desire, to fan the flame of creativity that will help us achieve our destinies.

I once read that Alexander the Great's mother, Olympias, repeatedly told Alexander that he was the son of a god. She believed that there was more in him, and she wanted him to be the man she told him he was. Our parents' guide us in that defining moment when we realize who we were born to be.

I can trace my defining musical moment back to one day in 1979 at Millwood Elementary School. On that day, what I decided my destiny would be, also started my downfall. My teacher, Mr. Leach, was the favorite teacher among all students. Besides being the only male teacher, boys like myself thought he was super cool. He was a handsome and rugged man, and the lady teachers always wanted to be around him. He was handsome because he always wore the best clothes and the most colorful shirts. Each shirt had various patterns of paisley, complete with a butterfly collar which was the cornerstone of 1970's style. He was rugged, because he had these big pork-chop sideburns that stretched from the bottom of his ear for at least four inches down his jaw line. As a result of years of smoking, his voice was deep and sounded like rocks grinding together. On occasions in class, he would hit himself in the chest just hard enough to make smoke rings come out of his mouth, which would solicit a chorus of ooh's and aah's from his fourth-grade class.

The day I thought I found my destiny, Mr. Leach informed us that we would be going to an assembly in the library. We followed quietly in a single-file line with our hands by our sides. The only sound was the loud swishing of corduroy pants as we made our way down the hall. While walking, I reached out my right hand and dragged my finger along the tile walls. The coolness of the tile always felt good on the hot summer days. As I walked, I hummed my own tune to the rhythmic bumps as my finger went over each grout line.

I had always liked music, but my knowledge was limited to what my mom and dad would listen to. Besides a steady diet of 70's radio and the Gaither Vocal Band, my parents had very few records. To say my musical influence was limited would be an understatement. In my house we were limited to bands like the Andrews Sisters, and Spike Jones or maybe Herb Alpert and the Tajuana Brass or Linda Ronstadt. They were my only outlet to modern music. I never would have anticipated the change that was about to take place in my life that day.

As we approached the library, I could see little plastic chairs had been set up in neat rows, each colored chair systematically corresponding with the row assigned to the grade that would be sitting there.

As we took our seats, our principal, Mr. Girvin gave us updates on school news and told us that we would be watching a film about the dangers of drugs on our society. He handed out brochures to give to our parents when we got home later that day that explained the film we were about to watch and included talking points for parents and kids on the dangers of drugs. The projector hummed and sputtered to life as it cast the picture on the far wall of the library, causing a hush to fall over the crowd.

The first thing I saw was video footage of Tom Shultz from the rock band Boston. He flung his hair around on stage and played the opening guitar chords of a song called "Smoking." Although I never saw his face, his presence was commanding, and his stature larger than life. His fingers were a blur across the fretboard that made a sound like grinding machinery that continued to build to a fever pitch resembling a Boeing 747 about to take flight. The lyrics that followed the opening guitar riff told me what I needed to do in life.

"Smoking, Smoking, come on now and keep on toking."

It was the greatest sound I had ever heard in my young nine-year-old life. The movie played more music by newly discovered influencers like Jimmy Hendrix, Jackson Browne, and Eric Clapton, whose lyrics taught me that "If I wanna hangout, I've got to take her out, Cocaine."

The assembly did not have the effect the teachers wanted it to have on me. I never even heard the message about the dangers of drugs, just the awesomeness that is Rock and Roll. I returned to class that day a different person. Dragging my finger on that tile was now different. I now had lyrics to go with the rhythmic beat of the grout lines. To the horror of my teacher, I sang the Jackson Browne song I had just learned softly to myself as we walked the hall, "Cocaine, you're all around my brain."

On the bike ride home that afternoon, I gave great thought to what I had perceived would be my musical destiny. The irony was that there was nothing wrong with Rock and Roll, but it would carry a lot of baggage. That baggage was the sex and drugs that came with it. The poor choices I would make in the years that followed would alter my musical destiny greatly.

I never gave that drug brochure to my parents. I dropped it on the side of the road on my bike ride home. Instead, I asked my dad if he could buy me a guitar. I knew that Rock and Roll would be my life and everything that went along with it. Rock and Roll would be my gateway drug to a much more powerful world of music, and that would be the world of heavy metal.

If you know anything about preacher's kids, they can be the worst ones. I was already heading down a wrong path. I would encounter many people throughout my life, and many would make a significant impact on it.

When I was still in the fifth grade, I met a guy named Ira Bacon at the fishing spot down the street at the second mill spillway. He was older, and we started hanging out a lot. He thought it was funny to teach a ten-year-old the F-word, and I wanted to impress him, so I used it a lot. He brought cigarettes and I would try one from time to time. He could also get his hands on some Busch beer. Not one person at the spillway seemed to mind a ten-year-old drinking beer. Just like the incident under the bridge with the cop and matches, those were just different times.

I got my first guitar and amp at twelve years old, and I joined a band called Blitzkrieg. The band members were Tom Cook on drums, his brother Todd on lead guitar, and James Gurney on bass. I was so excited to join as the rhythm guitarist and I was also the youngest in the group by a year, and James was about five years older than me. I was still trying to play the part of a Christian, but it was all a façade. As a band, we would do the things that we thought people wanted to see and hear like talk about God and sing about Him in our music, but we kept doing what we wanted to behind the scenes.

One night, the band members attended an event at the Sumter County Convention Center. Besides the annual Sumter High School graduations and the occasional county fair, not much went on there. The center's claim to fame was that Hank Williams Jr., in a drunken performance, pushed his piano off the stage, or so the legend would have it. But the name of the speaker at the convention center that night was Mike Warnke from Mike Warnke Ministries. He was to be an ex-navy corpsman from Vietnam, a drug dealer, hippie, and satanic high priest. His life had been changed by the Holy Spirit, and he was now spreading the Word of God around the country.

I recall that night questioning myself on where my life was heading and what direction I would go in. This was not my first encounter with Jesus and would not be my last. My life and God's will for me crossed paths regularly, but I always seemed to be going my own way.

But encouragingly, I wasn't the only one this was true about. Simon Peter also had several encounters with Jesus over the first year of Jesus' ministry.

JOHN 1:35-42

[35] *Again the next day after John stood, and two of his disciples;*

[36] *And looking upon Jesus as he walked, he saith, Behold the Lamb of God!*

[37] *And the two disciples heard him speak, and they followed Jesus.*

[38] *Then Jesus turned, and saw them following, and saith unto them, What seek ye? They said unto him, Rabbi, (which is to say, being interpreted, Master,) where dwellest thou?*

[39] *He saith unto them, Come and see. They came and saw where he dwelt, and abode with him that day: for it was about the tenth hour.*

[40] *One of the two which heard John speak, and followed him, was Andrew, Simon Peter's brother.*

[41] *He first findeth his own brother Simon, and saith unto him, We have found the Messias, which is, being interpreted, the Christ.*

[42] *And he brought him to Jesus. And when Jesus beheld him, he said, Thou art Simon the son of Jona: thou shalt be called Cephas, which is by interpretation, A stone.*

John the Baptists follower Andrew has gone out and brought his brother Simon Peter, to introduce him to Jesus. He tells his brother "We have found the Messiah, who is by interpretation the Christ." Peter meets Jesus for the first time, Jesus not only knows who he is, but also gives him a pretty cool nickname, Cephas. We would all assume that this was the life changing event that would forever change Peters course in life. But in Mark 1:16-17 it says,

MARK 1:16-17

[16] *Now as he walked by the sea of Galilee, he saw Simon and Andrew his brother casting a net into the sea: for they were fishers.*

[17] *And Jesus said unto them, Come ye after me, and I will make you to become fishers of men.*

Now by the Sea of Galilee, Simon Peter and Andrew are back at their jobs of fishing and get asked to "Be fishers of men," to be followers of Jesus. Jesus himself has a different job plan for Peter, but he uses an analogy Peter would understand which was fishing.

MARK 1:29-32

29 And forthwith, when they were come out of the synagogue, they entered into the house of Simon and Andrew, with James and John.

30 But Simon's wife's mother lay sick of a fever, and anon they tell him of her.

31 And he came and took her by the hand, and lifted her up; and immediately the fever left her, and she ministered unto them.

32 And at even, when the sun did set, they brought unto him all that were diseased, and them that were possessed with devils.

At this point, Jesus is at the house of Peter and heals Peter's mother-in-law. Jesus and Peter now know each other more, and Peter seems to be dedicated more to Him. But then, again, they have an encounter later in the book of Luke at a third location.

LUKE 5:1-11

1 And it came to pass, that, as the people pressed upon him to hear the word of God, he stood by the lake of Gennesaret,

2 And saw two ships standing by the lake: but the fishermen were gone out of them, and were washing their nets.

3 And he entered into one of the ships, which was Simon's, and prayed him that he would thrust out a little from the land. And he sat down, and taught the people out of the ship.

4 Now when he had left speaking, he said unto Simon, Launch out into the deep, and let down your nets for a draught.

5 And Simon answering said unto him, Master, we have toiled all the night, and have taken nothing: nevertheless at thy word I will let down the net.

6 And when they had this done, they inclosed a great multitude of fishes: and their net brake.

7 And they beckoned unto their partners, which were in the other ship, that they should come and help them. And they came, and filled both the ships, so that they began to sink.

8 When Simon Peter saw it, he fell down at Jesus' knees, saying, Depart from me; for I am a sinful man, O Lord.

9 For he was astonished, and all that were with him, at the draught of the fishes which they had taken:

10 And so was also James, and John, the sons of Zebedee, which were partners with Simon. And Jesus said unto Simon, Fear not; from henceforth thou shalt catch men.

11 And when they had brought their ships to land, they forsook all, and followed him.

Some scholars may say that Mark's fishers of men story and Luke's fishing story are the same.

The only thing similar is the mention of fishing for men. But there is one glaring difference. In Mark's version, he makes no mention of the miracle of the multitude of fish being caught and the moment Simon Peter repents in the boat. If it's the same story, I find it hard to believe that Mark would forget this major detail, especially since what Mark writes is also believed to be the account from Simon Peter himself, but that's my opinion.

The reason I bring these scriptures up is this. We will hear the testimony from our brothers about Jesus. That brother will bring us to introduce us to the Messiah. We will hear His call in our lives, Jesus will know us and name us. But many of us will go back to fishing, because in our own little worlds, we have jobs to do, we have a wife and family to care for. Jesus even heals Peter's mother-in-law and shows again that He will provide, that Peter need not worry. Repeatedly, the lives of Jesus and Peter cross paths.

Until we truly are moved by the Spirit and realize that because of sin we can't do it on our own, until we truly repent before Him, we will not be fulfilled. Ask yourself if fishing is where Jesus wants you to be. (Men you know what I mean...) Fishing is not wrong, but maybe he wants you somewhere else, doing His work in another field He has chosen for you.

That night at the convention center, Mike Warnke was my "Andrew." He introduced me to a whole new life I could have through God's grace. I got water sprinkled on my head as a baby and went through a lot of the motions growing up in the church. I knew about Jesus, and I knew that He knew me and named me, but that night I would choose to go back to fishing, back to my normal life, just like Peter did. Jesus would approach me over and over throughout my life, but it would take years of stumbling around and the direct intervention of an angel to see that my net was already full. Only then would I get on my knees in my boat of life and repent.

After listening to Mike Warnke's testimony and feeling God moving in my life, I wanted to make a change. The band and I left the Sumter County Coliseum with a new path and hope for our lives, one with purpose, and with a future. We wanted to rock out for Jesus. I felt that with my new-found direction, I was surely on the path towards fulfillment. What I did not realize was that the devil was waiting for me in the parking lot, and I did in fact take the new path, but the wrong one.

My friends and I changed the name of the band from "Blitzkrieg," the German name for lighting war from World War II to a more fitting name of "Blessed Knights." That way, the logo BK could stay the same on our stage banner and bass drum.

(Photo taken from the author)
James Gurney, Steve Gant, Todd Cook, Tom Cook.

We would become a "Christian-based" rock band. To this day I still do not truly understand the "based" part. Are we Christian, or are we not? You could compare it to, "This movie is based on a true story," meaning the story is not completely true but loosely based on facts that are. It started out in truth and meant well, but as time passed, we changed it around to spice it up a little. We were just the same product inside but with a new packaging.

Grinding it out in music was fun. Year after year, playing in the garage or the basement, trying to get to the next level. I admit that we had some stellar music, and our plan started out with the best intentions, but we went slightly off course. We played a few shows, but to mostly the other bands and their girlfriends that would attend.

We played a show at a church youth camp in Bon Clarken, NC. We drove all the way from Sumter, SC, to set up in a coffee shop setting and play about five songs. It was the first real show we had done; we spent all our money getting there, and it was awesome! Afterwards a girl from Lancaster, SC came up to me and asked me my name and if I wanted to go out some time, Wow! My first groupie! I was hooked.

On our way home from the show, the car had transmission problems and would not go over 40 mph. Nothing draws more attention on the highway than a car loaded with guys and band equipment, moving at 40 mph with smoke pouring out the windows. We would sing about God on stage and afterwards would smoke cigarettes, drink beer, and hang out with girls. I loved the Rock and Roll lifestyle and the girls that came along with it. That girl from Lancaster came to Sumter to hang out with me once, and that was another step to my view on women becoming distorted. I used her as a means to an end, and she wanted to use me to get out of her dead-end life.

We loved to play music, but it was hard to find places to play in such a small town. The only practice place we really had was the basement of

Tom and Todd's house. We would play day after day and all hours of the night. I remember sitting in that basement, chain smoking and writing music for hours. I would come up from the basement and find Todd and Tom's mother, Mrs. Cook, sitting at the kitchen table, smoking cigarettes, and reading the Bible at 2:00 AM. When I slept over, I would sit with her at the kitchen table late into the night, smoking cigarettes and talking to her about the scriptures and what they meant. I always appreciated her dedication to the study of His Word and how much she would put into it. She was never really one for organized religion; she would always say that all those people just keep getting in the way of each other, drowning out what God's trying to tell you. She had no problem sharing the Word of God with anyone and loved sharing her views on it.

After a while, the practice sessions moved from the basement to a more permanent place, the rental storage unit out on the Highway towards Shaw Airforce Base. That was where some of the real parties began. It was the same kind of rental storage units you now see all over the US. We rolled up the door, pulled the couch out into the driveway area between the units and played every song we wrote, smoking and drinking with girls and rocking out. Sometimes we drew a crowd, and we would party. My dreams of playing on the big stage of life was replaced with a storage facility. My life would become one big band practice/jam session in a rented warehouse off the highway. This went on for a few years and always ended with a drive down the strip, from the Piggly Wiggly parking lot to the Burger King parking lot and back.

During those late nights, my parents never seemed to overreact when it came to the lifestyle choices I was making. They always seemed so in control, or, as I would later find out, project the illusion of control. Instead of trying to control us, they gave that control over to the One that could control it. Rather than reacting with a heavy hand, my parents prayed for me daily.

The fact is that we believe we can have control when we should give that control to Jesus. Now I am not saying put on a blindfold and chuck life's steering wheel out the window. I am saying to put on God's glasses, which is His will, and put the steering wheel in God's hands. Do not let God be your co-pilot any longer but give God the wheel in all situations. Everything happens for a reason, and prayer will always cover your worries and fears.

There is a popular saying today that we see all over bumper stickers and window decals: "Never give up." This has become a battle cry for many on the frontlines of the world today, even many Christians. I admit that, when used, it gives people hope and strength to move forward, but here is the truth. We need to give up, give in, and give it to God. Wave the white flag and surrender to Him, because there is no other way to fight your battles than on your knees. We worry so much, and we try our best to carry the burden on our own. Our bodies and minds are not meant to carry such a load. We will break down, and we must learn to give it away to God. We must go to Him and continue to stay with Him. The same is true with the saying many people try to tell me: "God will never give you more than you can handle." The truth is, He does give us more, but He also gives us a way, and His name is Jesus.

Most grownups would tell you today, "I wish I would have listened to my parents when I was growing up." Oh, I listened to them, I just chose not to apply it most of the time. Now that I'm a parent too, I can tell my own parents thank you for the lessons they taught me. Even when I rolled my eyes, I was listening, just not applying it yet. I would continue this cycle of advice with my own children. Are they listening? Are they paying attention? I did not know then, but scripture says,

"Train up a child in the way he should go, and when he is old he will not depart from it."
Proverbs 22:6

Whether in my spiritual walk or personal life, I always remembered how my father had trained me up as a child, but I never could take that last step and stand for something. I was always in the boat of life, but never chose to get on my knees and repent. I went wherever the wind of the world would take me, and very quickly it began to feel like a hurricane.

Lord, Thank you for my unique upbringing. Thank you for the people you placed in my life that trained my up both spiritually and professionally. Thank you for always being there even when I did not see you or acknowledge you.

Chapter 2

GOD'S TIMING IS NEVER OFF.

"The definition of insanity is doing the same thing over and over and expecting different results."

–Albert Einstein

AS I REACHED high school, the next four years were pretty sketchy and could have gone extremely bad. The years from middle school through high school are volatile in a teen's life. Somehow common sense takes a complete leave of absence, and fortune-cookie living takes over. I really thought I knew better than my parents—it makes me laugh out loud today. It was like a complete lobotomy was done on me, and I do not know what happened.

I was still smoking and hanging out with people I thought were my friends. Yes, back then, there was no legal age for smoking. You could buy cigarettes at any store, and we even had a student smoking area at our high school. You had to have a slip signed by your parents, but that last part never really mattered, because no one ever checked them, and like mine, they were mostly all forged.

I tried to be liked by all the cool kids, or people I thought were cool. One day I brought two sixteen-ounce Budweiser Tall Boys to my gym class in my bag. I pulled one out in the locker room and showed some of the guys. I gave one to a group, and they started sharing it between the five of them. I then took out the other one, opened it, and drank it down right in front of them, finished it, and crushed it. I was the coolest guy ever.

We walked out of the locker room and into the gym and started to stretch, then divided up for basketball and began to play. This day was different because, whether I could play or not, I was quickly picked by the cool kids' team, finally! I had never been picked first for anything. They inbounded the ball to me, and I dribbled it down the court. I swear to this day that I was running straight, I bounced the ball like a pro and then ran right into the front row of the bleachers. The guys thought it was hilarious, that I was a clown. The coach came over and looked at me like I was an idiot and told me to sit down. He had to smell the beer on me, but to this day, he never said anything.

This would not be my first run in with alcohol at school. Later that same year, I had brought a liter of Lord Calvert whisky in my backpack, which I took from an older friend in the band I played in. I told some friends in the smoking area that I had it, and we made plans to meet up later. We agreed that we would meet in the bathroom after lunch to drink it before typing class. We drank it all. I believe I drank most of it to try to show off. All I remember was walking into typing class, sitting down, and hearing the bell ring to start class. I stared at the teacher as she spoke and thought how funny her face looked.

The next thing I knew the bell rang again, and everyone grabbed their bags and headed for the next class. The entire hour had gone by, and I do not think I even blinked my eyes. I went to English class and sat for a while, then raised my hand and asked to go to the bathroom. As I walked down the hall, it took every bit of mental strength just to walk straight. All I needed to do is sit down for a while, I thought. But as I crossed the upper mezzanine outside, I puked over the second-floor railing onto the flower bed below. I did this in full view of about six sets of classroom windows, both first and second floor. Not one person said anything to me or came outside, as if I was invisible. I really to this day believe I was.

I went to find a place to sit down and rest. The next thing I remember was someone waking me up. It was a cheerleader from the school. She was like an angel looking down on me. I was happy to be talking to her because she was someone that would never be seen talking to a person like me.

"Are you okay?"

I replied as cool as I could. "I'm fine."

She leaned down to whisper in my ear, "Are you drunk?"

I leaned in close enough to kiss her, and I even thought about doing it. "Why? Is that a problem?"

"Umm yeah," she whispered. "You're sitting in a chair right outside the head principal's office, and he's in there." She pointed at the open door.

Leave it to me to find a place to rest right outside the principal's office, drunk. She quickly got me up and took me down the hall and into the boy's bathroom. She sat me in the stall and told me to stay there until school was over.

I had no idea how long I was in there, but I listened to her and made it out unharmed. I made it to the bus and all the way home and slept the rest of the afternoon. I still cannot understand how no one noticed me. My parents didn't even think it was strange that I slept the rest of the day, just figured it was typical teenage behavior. When I saw the cheerleader a few weeks later in the hall, our eyes locked, and I got a smile from her. It was worth it. I started to try to straighten myself out. Besides the occasional class cutting and smoking pot, I believed I was making good progress.

When I was sixteen, I was dating a girl named Cathy who was thirteen at the time, and things seemed to be going well. It all started when I dropped off my friend Wade at his house after school, and his sister Cathy was shooting hoops in the driveway. One day she gave her brother a note to give to me, which he reluctantly did. That began a dating relationship that ended with me trying to sneak into her bedroom one night and getting caught. That also ended Wade's and my friendship forever. I learned to never date your friend's sister if you want to remain friends.

My bad behavior had finally come to a head, and after the sneaking out incident, my dad took me to Camden Military School in South Carolina to take a tour of my "possible future." After the tour, I told my dad that it had worked, and I would be on the straight and narrow from now on. I made one last ditch effort and convinced my dad to trust me and give me another chance. I told him I did not think the military life was really for me, something that I now, as a twenty-year Navy Veteran, find funny.

Sadly, I continued my destructive habit of selfish behavior, taking what I wanted and using people to get what I wanted. I knew I needed to head in a better direction. God kept calling, but I kept fishing my own way.

GODLY INTERVENTION

One of my great pleasures in life is to reason, study, and try to understand why things happen and how they work. As early as I can remember, I liked to take things apart and see how they work. I liked to solve complex problems whether it was human, or engineering. When it comes to engineering, machinery, or construction, I have always had the ability to understand and repair things. It might have come from all those years of watching *The Little Rascals* or Bob Villa do home repairs on his show, *This Old House*. Besides my parents, one man did see potential in me, who would fuel my love for building. His name was Mr. Ellis Oates.

When I was attending Sumter High School, half of my junior and senior years were spent at the Sumter County Career Center in Mr. Oates' Building construction class. We were taught framing, roofing, and all the aspects of construction. This was no shop class building bird houses, but a full-blown course on building houses. Mr. Oates, a retired Air Force veteran, showed me from the very beginning that I had an ability to not only work with my hands, but I could also do the book work and conquer my enemy, which was math.

When I was at the career center, I looked forward to going to his class and just having him teach me. He knew my grades were not good, but he showed me I could apply myself and do better. I firmly believe the guidance of Mr. Oates, the grace of God, and prayers from my parents drove me the last few years. I had the highest average in his class, and I pushed myself to be the best at everything I did.

At that time, I had a steady girlfriend named Shannon. I was trying not to bounce around from girl to girl and was doing my best to straighten myself out. My focus was to get a good job, find a good girl, and marry her. The job part of my life plan started to take shape in the form of construction. During my senior year, I was chosen to represent the Sumter County Career Center at the regional level in the building construction competition. Eight students from different vocational schools competed in a construction contest to see who would go to compete at the state level.

That Saturday, Mr. Oates drove me to the competition, and on the drive to Dillan, SC, we talked about school and his time in the Air Force. He told me the Air Force helped shape him and his future, and that after he retired, he wanted to continue to serve others by teaching. When we arrived at the facility, I could say I was a little nervous and not sure if I would be good enough. As the students gathered for the briefing and to go over the rules, the teachers began to gather and talk shop.

We were instructed to build the framing for the corner of a house. Two walls, 18" on center, 10' x 8' each, to include a corner post, a framed window to a set size, and a roof with hip rafters. All that using a pencil, tape measure, hammer, handsaw (no power), framing square, and nails. We were given a set amount of materials and would be judged by how much materials were left over. If we measured wrong or cut two pieces from the wrong stock, we would run out.

The teachers were taken into the next room and the students were told we had three hours to complete the task. As I viewed the materials, I could see the layout and understood it. I do not remember much of what happened but remembered it being fun. When I completed the construction, I looked it over and put down my hammer and walked out of the room. As I walked into the next room, I saw the teachers who were sitting in a circle of desks, drinking coffee, and shooting the breeze. All of them turned and looked at me as I came in.

Mr. Oates said, "Stephen, what happened? Are you okay?"

I replied, "No sir, I'm good. I finished my project."

He looked at the clock and it had only been an hour and thirty-five minutes of the three hours. The smile on his face was so big as he turned to the other teachers, he had to hide it with his coffee cup.

I walked up and just sat down next to him. He asked if I wanted some coffee and I said "Sure."

After the judging was completed, I was off on materials by 1 ½ inches and the only one to complete the project in the allotted time. I won a tool bag with all the framing tools and a Black & Decker power saw I would use for many years after that. I went on to place third out of twenty in the state competition at the Columbia fairgrounds that year. I learned to never judge myself compared to what others do, to never try to put limitations on myself or try to put myself in a box.

To complete a project in half the time became normal for me. I started to learn that you should never allow someone to put limitations on you, and you should do all you can to shatter expectations. If someone had told me I have three hours to complete this and had added, "by the way, most will never finish it," I might have approached it a little differently. I might have been a little more cautious in my work. But as it turned out, I knew I never wanted to put myself in a box ever again, never place limits on my God-given ability. This way of thinking would take me through the rest of my life. God had shown me that there are no limits when He gives you your abilities.

Mr. Oates taught me that when we take the time to see potential in others, it is our job as leaders to help them realize that potential. There is nothing more frustrating than a man that does not know his purpose in life. Mr. Oates had the key and taught me to believe in myself and that one man can make a difference in a life. The impact it had on me lasted a lifetime. He would be the first of many to teach me this.

When it came to my relationships, the train had derailed. I had broken up with my girlfriend

Shannon and started to date Tara, who was still in high school, and we were not walking the way we should have. When it came to my work life, things seemed to be shaping up nicely. I was offered an opportunity to work at a construction project for Flour Daniels Construction at the Union Camp Paper Mill Phase II in Eastover, SC. Eastover is about an hour drive from my house and halfway between Sumter, SC, and the Capital of Columbia. It is not very big and for good reason. Paper mills back in the day smelled a lot like sewage plants. The smell of wet pulp was unmistakable. The smell I brought home would knock you over in a minute.

The pay was good; I was making about $10.00 an hour in 1990, which was above average for a nineteen-year-old. When I had applied for the job, my mom's brother, Uncle David, who also worked for the company, had put in a good word for me. Family or not, I was ready to get there and show them the construction ability God had given me. Driven to succeed, I would be setting the standard for performance.

I showed up on the job sight with another 1,000 men, all standing in line. One guy in line looked at my clean-cut look, new lunch cooler, tool belt, and hammer and asked, "What did your mom pack in your lunch, kid?"

I mean, you could still smell the new leather on my tool belt; it was like blood in the water around a school of sharks. Not being mean, but first day hazing had begun. As we waited, the same guy gave me some good advice. Keep out of people's way, work just hard enough to not get fired, but slow enough not to work yourself out of a job. But most importantly: do not piss off iron workers, or you could be in for a long fall.

Surrounded by all the new workers, I was called into the office of Dave Cleveland, who was the senior project manager, head honcho, and our boss. He introduced himself told me and that he knew my Uncle David and had heard about me. We exchanged small talk and he told me I would be assigned to a crew ran by a guy named Fred Lewis, and that he would look after me.

As I left his office, he shook my hand and said, "if you talk to your Uncle David, tell him I said hi."

As I turned around, everyone in ear shot heard him. So much for low profile. The last thing you wanted on a job like this was to be a brown noser.

In this construction world, I would learn some valuable lessons, some easy and some hard. In these types of construction projects, they had 1,000 plus men at any time. When the work slowed down, some workers would move on to the next job or as we called it "drag up," which meant you got your tools and hit the gate. They would then travel to the next job and live in some shady motel, the weekly rate places you usually see on the highway. Most men were card-carrying members of the company and had worked on other jobs with Flour Daniels before.

I was a minnow in an ocean of men. I was no longer a standout but another face in the crowd. God-given ability or not, it would be hard to shine in this group. Humble would be my pie, and it looked good. I admit it was a little depressing at first, but I wanted to keep my head down, not make a mistake, and piss someone off. Low profile was ok for me.

During the next two years I would work for some of the craziest people I ever met. Troy Bunch, who cursed like a sailor and often told off-color jokes. Weldon was a carpenter with a leg injury from Vietnam. Frank, who was Weldon's best friend and drinking buddy. Bob Fisher, nicknamed Pastor, who would talk about Jesus every chance he got. Melvin, the only black man I worked with and who was the crew's welder. This was the largest-scale job I had seen so far in my life. It had so many levels and people, like an ant hill someone just kicked over.

My job on the construction crew was a lot of grunt work. One of my biggest tasks was to keep supplies moving from area to area and keep up with the carpenters by nailing as fast as I could. Amy, a fork truck driver who chain smoked and had a Harley Davidson tattoo on her forearm, would be one of my best contacts and kept me on schedule with supply moves. I became a master at being resourceful, a quick thinker, and slick talker. When I needed something moved quickly, I would go to Amy and ask for her help. She would smile and say, "I'll be right there baby." On the construction site, there was no such thing as sexual harassment. I really think Amy liked me because she asked me out a few times to get a beer, which was kind of creepy because she was like forty and I was nineteen.

Melvin would teach me how to weld, so I could fill in for him sometimes. Nothing complex, just spot-welding pieces together to set the level for the concrete to be poured. When Melvin got married, I was the welder while he was out for the week. Welding was fun and something new.

Pastor Bob would talk about Jesus and His saving grace all day. He could literally bring up Jesus in any conversation and talk to anyone. He always invited me to go to the prison in Columbia with him to preach the Word on Sundays, and I would kindly decline. I could never imagine myself ever visiting a prison, which is funny now that I think about that also.

I had been there about two years and seemed to be settled in relatively well when a chain of events started that would change everything.

One day, while working on pouring concrete, a horn sounded, and Weldon grabbed his toolbox and yelled at me. "Grab your tools Spiky!" They called me that because I had cut my hair so it would stand up and look like a mohawk. I was in that phase when I cared about impressing others.

I asked Weldon, "Why are we leaving?"

"A laborer just fell and died. Everyone's got to get off the job site, because you do not want to be around for the investigation."

I was shocked. A laborer was the guy who swept and cleaned job sites and did unskilled labor. This was the first time I had seen someone dead, so it was a little strange. At a funeral viewing the person is all fixed up and looking natural. But seeing this guy lying there after falling four stories was not natural. His legs were not in the right place and should never have bent that way.

A few months later another laborer was cleaning the sixth floor right before they were to pour concrete. He picked up a piece of plywood and walked forward, sliding the plywood, and not knowing that it covered a hole. I watched him fall through that hole and I heard him hit the ground. Before I even had a chance to say anything, Weldon yelled, "Grab your belt!" and with that we were done for the day. Death happens at this type of job, and you had to watch your step. I had heard of guys that get blown off the high steel at these places. It is the last place you want to be when you are not paying attention or on drugs.

Drugs were not a serious problem as far as I could tell, but they were around, and you would hear about them. During this time at Flour Daniels, I split rent with another guy from the job.

We rented part of the house from a friend, and it turned out he was addicted to crack cocaine. One night, he asked if I wanted some, I told him no. That living arrangement did not last long, and neither did he at work. I know it was not a smart decision to room with a known crack head, and neither was lending my twelve-gauge pump shotgun to a coworker, but it seemed like a good idea at the time.

Cliff was one of my many African American friends at the job site. I had known Cliff for a few months and was giving him a ride to work almost every day; in return he would buy the coffee. One Friday afternoon, Cliff and his brother said that they were going to go hunting that weekend and asked to borrow my shotgun. I thought, "well why not?" I gave him the gun and never thought twice about it. I came to pick him up for work that Monday, honked the horn, and he did not come out. I went up and knocked on the door, and his wife told me he wouldn't be going to work for a while. She proceeded to tell me the story that he and his brother had robbed a liquor store Friday night, using my shotgun. I never saw Cliff, or the shotgun, again. I was growing wiser by the day.

A few weeks later, Weldon had come into work and told me Frank Hill, his best friend and drinking buddy, had been shot and killed the night before. Frank was at the home of a girl he met at a bar, and he was shot while climbing out the window by her husband who came home early. That day, the crew grabbed their tools and headed for the gate. After cashing my check, we ended up at a little bar in Eastover drinking beer and playing pool with some of the guys. Our foreman, Fred Lewis told me things were slowing down at the job and they were thinking about dragging up for good. He asked if I wanted to come with him and his daughter to Texas to work another job site. I seemed to be fitting in quite well at the job site, so it was a possibility. I was making some good progress, learning a lot, and making good money. I had some time under my belt and could breeze right into the next job.

Fred explained that he lived with his daughter, who also worked at the job site. They both lived in a small silver pull-behind trailer, and he said I could stay with them. He and his daughter had lived and traveled in that trailer for about eight years, working from job to job.

At the bar that afternoon, I reflected on the last two years and all the things that went wrong, the deaths, the drama, and the drugs. I asked myself the question, why was all of this happening? I was still playing in the band, but my girlfriend Tara and I had broken up, and I was back on my own. Tara and I had dated for two years, and I had always thought she was the one. I seemed to sabotage every relationship I was in. I had the job, but still not the girl. I knew this decision could very well change the course of my life forever, and I needed to give it some serious thought. I left the bar, bought a six pack of Busch beer and a pack of cigarettes, and I thought about it on my hour drive home to Sumter. I was not leaving there empty handed. After about two years at Flour Daniels, I had learned to survive in a pack of wolves. I learned how I could push myself in resourcefulness and ingenuity. I learned to weld and engineer some pretty cool stuff. But I felt deep down, I was being pulled into another direction. I'm not sure if I was being guided, but sometimes you get that strong feeling inside that you were made for something bigger. I understood at that moment that I had had enough. I needed a safer job, because I still wanted to get a good job and get married. I would like to say I prayed about it, but I did not. After buying some more beer, I went to Dillon Ballpark and Recreation in Sumter and thought about what I wanted to do with my life. By the end of the ninth beer, I knew I would never go back to that job site in Eastover. I knew where I would go. I left the ballpark that minute, got in my car, and went straight to the Navy recruiter's office and joined the Navy.

Lord, thank you for always protecting and providing, even in the small things that might go unseen. For protecting me when I make poor decisions in life and still loving me when I fall short. Thank you for providing life opportunities to learn from and being there to help shape me in both the good and bad choices I made.

Chapter 3

A MATTER OF LIFE AND DEATH

I used to rule my world from a pay phone
And ships out on the sea
But now times are rough
And I got too much stuff
Can't explain the likes of me
–Jimmy Buffet

WHEN I LOOK BACK on that choice to go from the dangerous world of big-time construction to the United States Navy, it probably wasn't the safe choice at the time, but a choice had to be made. It may not seem rational now, but this change propelled me out of the dead-end life I was in. Like a choose-your-own-adventure book, where you make a choice at the end of a chapter, go to the chapter you selected, and see what happens. Sometimes the choices were successful, and in some you died.

I was at the end of a chapter and needed to choose a direction. I was contemplating moving into a pull behind trailer with a father and daughter construction team and live the life of a nomad. My biggest fear was that if I had said yes, my life would have become a blur of construction sites, hard drug use, and eventually dying in a Winnebago, desperate and alone.

I have learned that to break out of a routine, I have to make a radical change. It's not like I was foolishly seeking out danger by joining the Navy, but sometimes I did put myself in different situations, and without my knowledge, danger would find me.

JANUARY 18TH, 1991

When it came to joining the Navy, I was what the recruiters might call a dream recruit. Typically to get someone to join can be hard, phone calls, school visits, and numerous meetings. Rarely do people just walk into the office. I was educated, healthy, mostly drug free, and (the most important criteria) willing to join now. I never saw myself as the military type, but there I was in the recruiter's office. He handed me two tests, one in the form of a sheet paper, and the other was a cup with a lid.

He said, "You need to take these two tests. One you must pass. On the other one, just spell your name right."

In 1991, if you had a heartbeat and half a brain, you could join, but that has since drastically changed today. I told the recruiter I liked to work with my hands and was good at construction and welding. I also mentioned that I liked to cook, which was weird because my extent of cooking was fried bologna sandwiches or refrigerator chili, which is when you throw everything in your fridge into a pot of beans. I guess I imagined the Navy would send me to culinary school, which would have been fine with me. He informed me that I had a choice: I could sign up as a Mess Specialist (MS), which was a ship's cook, or a Hull Technician (HT), which was a steel worker and welder. I chose HT and I am glad I did.

A guy we called Byrd was a coworker at Flour Daniels and a cook in the Navy for a few years. Byrd told me that being a cook in the Navy can be rewarding, but the creativity was never there for them. There was no real culinary school just some basic skills. You pretty much just followed a recipe card and then stood in the serving line and listened to guys tell you how much you sucked at cooking.

I made the decision that would alter my future forever. I had joined the Navy and was ready to get on with my life. Now I just needed to tell my family and my new girlfriend, Stacey.

A week or so after I signed up, I was on my way to boot camp. My parents dropped me off at a hotel in Columbia, SC, outside Fort Jackson, where I would begin my long journey. It did not take long for me to be lied to for the first time. During in processing the next day, the admin clerk gave me my travel orders and airplane ticket.

I looked at it and said, "There must be a mistake. My recruiter told me I am supposed to be going to bootcamp in Orlando, FL, not Chicago!"

The admin clerk never even looked up from her work and replied with heavy sarcasm, "Your recruiter lied. How original."

Hours later, I landed in Chicago, IL, and was on a bus headed to Naval Training Center, Great Lakes, Ill in January. The bus driver told us, "Smoke as much as you can on the bus, because it will be the last time you will."

My plan was to blend in as much as I could, just like I did at Flour Daniels, and blend in I did. I stepped off that bus, and the first thing I felt was the crisp Chicago winter air and the drops of spit coming from a guy's mouth as he yelled, cursed, and referenced my mother a lot right in my face. They shaved our heads, took our clothes and any notion that we were special.

Boot camp went by like a blur. I attended chapel services on Sunday from time to time, not so much to worship, but to get a break from the daily life of the barracks. There was no real Christian influence to speak of while I was there except for some recruit getting the position of the religious leader of the company. This position usually involved escorting recruits to chapel and praying at night before lights out, which sometimes resulted in snide comments from others.

My Company Commanders were not religious at all. AME1 Dehine would refer to God but not in a holy way. He would mention God and prayer to us, but it was usually something like, "Gant! You better pray to God I don't come over there and stomp you into the ground." I spent nine weeks in the frozen tundra of North Chicago as an average recruit. I am serious; I was an average, run of the mill, regular guy.

Once I graduated, I went to the Naval Damage Control Training Center in Philadelphia, PA to attend Hull Tech "A" school. They taught us pipefitting, all levels of welding, drafting, lagging, handling sheet metal, ship fitting, and a few weeks of firefighting. It was a good time; we learned a lot, and the chow was pretty good at the Mess Hall.

We were also able to go out to the big city of Philly sometimes. The school was in the shadow of I-95 and across the street from the stadiums where the Eagles, Phillies, and Flyers would play. If we went to the games in uniform, we would get free tickets. We'd sometimes even make it to Cookies Bar in downtown Philly. Cookies was a little hole-in-the-wall bar owned by a retired Marine. We young guys could sit for hours, sipping on fifty-cent draft beers or, if we were feeling strong, do flaming shots of Sambuca. Sambuca was a liquor that tasted like black licorice and the alcohol content was high enough that you could light it on fire, and just before you drink it down you blow it out like a candle. Not timing it right or blowing it out too hard would burn a few hairs on my arm.

We would sit and listen to the old devil dogs relive the combat and Marine Corps days of old. I gained a lot of respect for the elders we were around, who took pride in sharing their stories. All they really wanted was to have someone listen and show them respect, because they deserved it. More than once, I stayed too late and even once passed out on the subway platform for a few hours, only to be roused by the police and sent back to the barracks. A drunk sailor on a subway platform in his dress whites was a common site.

Every other day we had to do physical training (PT). All students were ordered to show up for PT, and we would do warmups and run around the base, right past the rows of old ships in mothballs. These were old ships that had exceeded their service life on the sea, but the government preserves them for future use in case they need to be recalled to action. Some of the old DD's (Destroyers) and FF's (Frigates) were taken out of service, welded shut, and placed side by side, just in case. Like those old Marines sitting in that bar, those ships were waiting to be called on again, ready for action and had a million stories to tell if someone would just listen.

As a Hull Tech, I repaired ships for a living, and I knew that they take constant maintenance to keep them up even when you live onboard. I couldn't imagine what condition they had to be in after just sitting there in storage, but still, it was an awesome sight to see. So much Naval history and power in one place. We ran by the USS *Kitty Hawk*, who was in for maintenance for a few years. It was the first time I got to see an active aircraft carrier up close. I remember feeling the pride of what was to come, and I would get to live on something so massive and powerful.

As we finished our run around the base, the running course took us by the base's McDonalds. In the window, I saw students from my class waving at me, some of them laughing and giving me the finger. They were inside eating dinner before going out to the bar. When I spoke to them later at Cookies, they said, "No one ever checks, so you don't have to run."

I also wondered why no one ever checked. Why would you make a rule and not enforce it? We were 200+ students at the school, and fifty would show up to run. Why was no one holding us accountable? My dad had always told me that I should do the right thing even when no one is watching, so I ran each time, and I never missed a day.

The Navy life was easy. They fed me, gave me clothes to wear and a place to sleep. The best advice I got and would often pass on to other sailors was this, "Do what you are told, and you will survive. Do it before you are told, you will be a Master Chief." I was finally starting to mature a little every day and take responsibility for my actions. I would run simply because they told me too.

I started to understand more about being responsible and being a leader. I recalled what Mr. Oates was able to do with me. He took the time to see who I was and helped me unlock that gift I had buried down deep. Like the day I won the building competition in high school. I loved the feeling of being successful and living without limits put on me. I realized, as I ran that day, what I was called to do. I wanted to pour into others, unlock their gifts, and see them succeed. I even started to notice that when most people were just standing around, they wanted to do something, they were just waiting for someone to tell them what to do. These were men with a purpose, they just needed direction. So, I just started to speak up, people listened, and things would get done. My leadership focus and running seemed to be getting better, but my spiritual walk was nowhere to be found.

Now in Philadelphia HT "A" school, the higher the grades you got, the higher up on the list you'd be when picking orders of locations to be stationed. Getting a good location was a big deal. Grades determined if you would go to somewhere as cool as Hawaii or as bad as

Norfolk, VA. My Granddaddy Gant told me years ago that Norfolk is a hemorrhoid on the butt of the Navy, and I always remembered that. I pushed myself to be the best in my class and got second, one behind my roommate Shawn Carroll. When it came to orders, I chose USS *Frank Cable* AS-40, a submarine repair ship stationed in Charleston, SC. The irony is that I joined the Navy to see the world, and the first place I choose was my birthplace. The good news was that my roommate Shawn also chose the same location.

I reported to the USS *Frank Cable* AS-40 at Naval Station in Charleston. It was located right off Spruill Avenue by the waterfront. The crew numbered around 2,000, and I was assigned to the Sheet Metal Shop (17A). I spent six good years on that ship and learned a lot from so many people.

On my first day, I was given a tour of the ship by HT2 Joe Eastman, and on the tour, he made it a point to show me where the coldest drinking water on the ship was located, which was very high on his list of shipboard need to know. There were so many people on the *Frank Cable* that would influence my life in so many ways. My plan was to stay with the Navy as long as they would let me, and make as much money as I could. Maybe even retire and have a great pension. But just one year into my plan my old demons came back to visit me, and I put my entire plan in jeopardy by making a terrible decision.

I went to dinner at the home of one of my supervisors in the sheet metal shop. His wife cooked spaghetti. After dinner, they brought out some pot, lit up, and began to pass it around. I smoked pot with them that night while we watched TV. I regretted it to this day because that decision could have changed my entire future. For the next three weeks, I went into work every morning, paranoid because sometimes they would announce random urinalysis tests at quarters. If they had called my number, I would've been kicked out forever.

After sidestepping a few career landmines, I was doing my best to go in the right direction and not sabotage my future. So many people made a difference in steering my career, but the most important influence on that ship was my Leading Chief Petty Officer (LCPO), DCCS (SW) Leon Lantagne. Many nights, I would stand watch in Damage Control Central, and he would sit up with me for hours and quiz me on Fire Fighting and Damage Control procedures and equipment. These study sessions would take me to be one of the leading firefighters on the ship and the on-scene leader for the At Sea Fire Party (ASFP). The ASFP was a collection of the best firefighters on the ship that could respond at a moment's notice at any hour of the day or night. Senior Chief Lantagne set an example for me as a leader and mentor. He taught me to care for my men, to train them and show concern for them. Never ask them to do anything I wouldn't do myself. He taught me to "Set the bar high and lead them up and over it." Always talk highly of your men in other company and scold them in private, which was hard most times. Set the standard and hold others to it.

With his leadership and teaching, I was on the fast track. I pushed myself to never be afraid and to be the best at whatever I was doing. Those around me were steering me in a direction of excellence, but sadly I still did not listen for God. Despite all the great leadership examples I had and the oath I made to myself not to do drugs, the abuse of alcohol continued and even escalated.

Because Charleston Naval Shipyard was only about two hours away from home, a shipmate from Sumter, Jacob "Buddy" Cole and I would drive the hour and forty minutes home, sometimes twice a week, to see our girlfriends and turn around at 4AM and drive to work to make it on time. One afternoon, we got a bottle of whisky before driving home. I got to Stacey's moms house hammered drunk and passed out on the couch. I slept the entire time. The next thing I remembered was Buddy knocking at the front door to pick me up to drive back to the ship.

I drove back that night and at one-point lost my lighter in the car. Wanting to smoke a cigarette, I pulled over to the side of interstate 95 to look for it while Buddy slept. There I was, still drunk and digging around under my seat on the side of I-95 at 4:30AM. I could barely see anything except for the occasional headlight until the familiar red-and-blue lights filled the inside of the car. I explained to the police officer who we were and what had happened, and after studying us for some time he used his flashlight to find my lighter and told us to get moving. There was a healthy respect for the military uniform ever since the start of Desert Storm, but I was pushing it a little too far.

I came into work one morning and heard the rumor that an HT from the Nuclear Repair Shop had died last night at his home. There were a few hundred HT's onboard such a big ship, but, being an HT, I wondered who it was and if I knew him. I knew very few of the guys on the nuclear side because the security was so strict.

Shortly after our morning briefing, my Chief brought me into the Master Chief's office to talk. On most occasions this would've been a bad thing, and being only an E3 in the Navy, I was filled with terror. Being an E3 and going to see a Master Chief would hardly ever happen. As I walked into his office, I tried not to let my fear show. The Master Chief asked me if I knew of a Sailor named Shawn Carrol.

I said, "Yes, I went to bootcamp with him at Great Lakes and roomed with him in Hull Tech school." It then dawned on me that Shawn worked in R10 Nuclear side.

Master Chief then told me that Shawn had killed himself last night while arguing on the phone with his wife. He said that his wife could not go there, but they needed me to go to the trailer he lived in and identify that it was him.

On my way over I tried to figure out what had happened and struggled with why. When I arrived at his house, the police brought me inside. It was almost like a dream. It was so cold in there, I started to shake and was not sure if it was from the cold or the gravity of the situation. I had no idea what I was supposed to do. I had seen a dead body before but never from three feet away and especially not a friend. His head was covered with a sheet, and I was informed that facial recognition could not be used, but they asked if I could I help them anyway. I knew right away it was him from the tattoos that he had. I confirmed that it was him and I left that place as fast as I could.

Why was he dead? Why would he do that? The police said it was an alcohol-related incident. I knew that wasn't true because there was only one beer on the table, and the rest was in the fridge. I roomed with Shawn and drank with him. He was from Boston and was no slouch when it came to handling his booze. No way was one beer going to affect him in the slightest. Here was yet another death in the saga that was my life, and it was not the last. On my ride home that weekend, I wrote the lyrics and music for the song, "The Only Way" by the Blessed Knights. It was about suicide and how it affects the ones left behind.

Despite several missteps, I had survived the first couple years in Charleston. Deep down inside, I was looking for answers and direction. I knew I need something more, a better council to keep me going in the right direction. I needed someone to hold me accountable and push me along when I needed it. I decided the best and natural course of action was to marry my high school sweetheart, Stacey Meyer, and we moved to Hanahan, SC where we would live for the next 2 years.

My career seemed to flourish, and things really started to pick up when the announcement came that Charleston Naval Station was closing, and all the ships were being reassigned. I was concerned that we were going to be moving to Norfolk, VA. Norfolk was the last place I wanted to be. The official Naval message was released: USS *Frank Cable* was to be decommissioned. Wow! My first ship would be cut up into pieces and scrapped, or maybe if she was lucky, she'd be lined up with those retired ships in Philadelphia.

Using my learned resourcefulness, over the next six months, we started to take all the equipment off the ship and box it up or give it to any ship that needed it. Ships were coming over and asking for our old stuff, so we would just give it to them, write them a receipt on anything, and let them take it. As we were unloading everything, the report came out that the USS *Holland* in Guam was being removed from service. I remembered when the USS *Holland* had a small fire pier-side in Charleston. They took on repairs and had left for Guam just a short time before this. The word was, floating around the waterfront, that they were having serious problems. A naval message soon followed that we were to re-man the USS *Frank Cable*, get new equipment and a new crew, and move ourselves, our families, and our ship to Guam. Things never really turn out how we plan them. I have always been told, if you want to hear God laugh, tell Him your plans. On my way home I had to figure out how to tell Stacey we were moving to Guam, and, more importantly, I even had to figure out where Guam was located.

The Guam transition went about as well as expected. We left Charleston, SC, transited the Panama Canal, and crossed the Pacific Ocean with half the crew, a few fires, and some flooding issues. So, all in all, it was a good trip, and no one died.

Guam was paradise on earth. It was very tropical with beaches and waterfalls you'd see on a post card. It also had a darker past from being a battlefield during WWII. The scars were still there on the beaches and in the jungles, complete with bunkers dug into the coral walls that used to house machine-gun positions to repel offensive attackers on the beach head. They also still had old tanks in the fields, rusting into the ground or half-sticking out of the ocean waves, like they were gasping for their last breath of air. All over the island, you could hike to these places to see history or dive off the coast to see the many sunken ships or planes just littering the ocean floor.

The island of Guam could be heaven on earth to many sailors, but if the wrong decisions were made, it could be a dark hell. You either spent most of your time participating in the dozens of outdoor activities, or you were drinking in the dozens of bars. On all accounts, my career, my life, and my marriage seemed to be going right, but underneath the surface, the seams were starting to further unravel. Unlike what I had stated in my wedding vows, I was not able to forsake all others. Stacey and I had obvious problems, but instead of facing them, we filled our lives with all the distractions that the island would offer, such as camping, snorkeling, and drinking.

While in Guam, Stacey had become pregnant, and we were expecting our first child. Rather than focusing on my marriage, which I thought I had plenty of time for, I spent a lot of time in Japan or Korea with the *Frank Cable*, working on submarines that needed repairs. The times in Japan were spent working, drinking, and sometimes fighting. Sailors gathered at the end of the day at The Honch in Yokosuka, which was an area that contained one of the numerous "buy me drink" bars. Buy-me-drink bars were watering holes that Japanese girls would go to, and sailors would buy them drinks and hang out. It was mostly just harmless fun. You could be entertained just by trying to talk to a girl who does not understand English, or you could both participate in Japan's favorite past time, Karaoke.

In places like Popeye's in Yokosuka, drinks would flow, words would be exchanged, and tempers would flare. In the old Navy, it was okay to talk bad about your own ship, but you never let anyone from another ship talk bad about your ship, even if it was true. There was a lot of bad blood between the USS *Frank Cable* and the USS *Independence* that would often end in a barroom brawl, and in a place like Popeye's, a good brawl drastically improved the look of the place. It was a dump!

One day, in a phone booth in Sasebo, Japan, talking with Stacey back in Guam, she told me that she had gone to the doctor, and we were having twins!

I looked out the phone booth and saw my Command Master Chief walking by. I told him, "I'm having twins!"

He looked at me strangely and replied, "That's good Gant, Congratulations!"

I thought, twins... twins... I could barely take care of myself much less two kids. It was at that same moment I knew God had a sense of humor, and I was in deep trouble.

Everything seemed to be going quite well when I was back at home in Guam and life was good. Many weekends were spent camping on the beach with friends, snorkeling, and just hanging out. We played horseshoes in the back yard, and I believe we cooked on the grill almost every night.

I was on duty onboard the ship one night, and I had just come off watch and headed for my bunk to get some sleep. Duty is when a set number of people stay overnight on the ship to maintain minimum manning in case of an emergency such as fire or flooding. Even if the ship had to get underway quickly, we could start preparations while the crew was called in. My plans were to finish my duty day, make it to turnover in the morning at 0730 (7:30AM), pick up Stacey at home and to go to the Guam hospital. Stacey was due for a wellness check-up to see how the babies were doing and checking her due date.

I was awakened August 6th, 1997, around 02:30AM by the alarm bells being rung to respond to a fire or flooding. I jumped from my bunk and was putting on my coveralls and my boots, waiting to hear the details of what the nature of the disturbance was. The announcing system said to muster all fire party personnel to the mess decks.

The mess decks? Really? I quickly made my way to the crew's eating area. The section leader informed us that there was a plane crash on the island, and we would be going to the site to aid the local fire department where we could. We took some basic equipment, loaded a van, and started for the sight. We only took about ten personnel and some basic gear like pry bars, axes, and a few Army litter stretchers. Guam is about thirty miles long by eight miles wide, and it doesn't take long to get anywhere, especially at 3:30 in the morning. We made our way to the scene, debating what we would be doing, just guessing what had happened. I believed it was a small piper cub or private plane that carries about four people and was sometimes used by businessmen going to and from Japan or one of the surrounding islands in the Marianas chain. When we arrived at the site, we saw only one fire truck and that confirmed in my mind the idea of a single-engine, small plane crash.

We were briefed and went through the metal gate and started our walk along the ridge of a small hill. It was still pretty dark, and the small ridgeline dirt road led us to the beacon that guides planes to the runway. In fact, we could see the runway in the distance a few miles away, still lit up, and behind it the beautiful star-filled sky in the distance. Then suddenly I noticed the smell of fuel and smoke in the air. I had a stretcher over one shoulder, and my friend Jared Butler had the other end. We walked along the tree line until there were no more trees. I stood in amazement–all the remaining trees were broken off at the trunks and laid over like broken toothpicks. In place of the trees was an engine from a Boeing-sized jetliner still on fire. We looked over the ridge into the valley below, and there was Korea Air 801, cracked open like an egg with its contents spilled all over the place.

We were instructed to form a line an arm's length apart and walk down the embankment, through the waist-high razor grass to look for survivors and provide aid if we could. It was dark and hard to see, but if you hit something with your feet that was not razor grass, you bent down to see what it was. Sometimes it was debris, and sometimes it was someone, or what remained of someone. We found many people in the grass, but everyone I found was deceased. We attempted to place some on stretchers and carry them out, which proved to be difficult in such terrain. I was at the head end of a stretcher and going up the hill when I slipped and fell. I still held on while the stretcher hit me. The head of the deceased man bumped into mine, and his mouth landed against my ear. I heard him exhale the last bit of air that was trapped in his lungs into my ear. It still creeps me out today to think about it.

By this time, it was morning, and Stacey was up and had called her mom back home in SC. They were talking about the crash, which was now on the international news stations. Stacey told her mom that she had not heard from me and was not sure what was going on or where I was. This was well before cell phones and texting, and there was no payphone where I was. As she was still talking to her mom and watching the news, she told her mom, "I know where he is. He is at the crash site."

While she was speaking to her mom, she had seen my face on the news wearing my red ships ball cap from the fire party on the ship. It turned out that the flight was coming in for a landing at Guam Airport and had put the landing gear down. The low-level alarm was disabled because of the landing, and the pilot came in too low, clipping the tree line on the hill with the landing gear. Over the next few days, they would discover that the pilots had been flying too long and had become too tired to control the aircraft.

We spent most of the morning at the sight collecting bodies and tagging them. If they had an ID on them, we placed it in a bag on top of them. If they were still in a seat, we wrote the number on a tag and attached it to them for identity later. As I made my way to the main part of the plane, I could look inside and still see some of the people strapped into their seats, as if they were waiting for the plane to take off.

Several scenes from that day will be forever ingrained into my memory. One was, among all the scattered luggage, this one men's dress shoe. It was black and brightly polished, probably ready for a business meeting. It would not have seemed out of place if it hadn't been for the severed foot that was still wearing it. Another image was the inner wall of the plane. There was a section of the wall and window I could see so closely that I also saw the thousands of small, perforated holes in the metal. Each hole perfectly machined with precision and accuracy. That same wall section that was so meticulously made was also splattered with blood running down to the carpet.

I would see that wall pattern again about three months later. Jared Butler and I would board a Korea Air flight to Seoul, Korea. My gaze on that flight was transfixed on that pattern on the wall as we took off from Pusan and landed in Seoul. I could still see the blood on the wall and the faces that would never fly again. With the faint smell of jet fuel still in our nostrils, neither Jared nor I spoke much about it on the flight; we just kept completely silent.

Two years in Guam made it a great duty station, but after a total of six very successful years on the *Frank Cable*, I chose to move my career from fast track to the super speedway. I chose orders to Naval Station Great Lakes as a division commander. I was going back to boot camp not to be screamed at again, but I was going to do the yelling as an RDC (Recruit Division Commander) or commonly known as a drill instructor to the rest of the world. I got to yell as much as I wanted, I was good at it, and I loved it.

It was one of those jobs that I would have done for free. When it came down to playing good cop/ bad cop with recruits, I liked to be the bad one. I was known as someone who would just as well choke you to death than talk to you. Firm but fair would be my motto. No question about it, this would be the high point of my career. I was up at 4:00AM and sometimes home by 10:30PM. I would tell myself daily that if I got to the next level in the Navy, I could provide more for my family. I told myself that I was doing this all for my wife and my family because they deserved the best, and I would give it to them.

Just weeks after I reported to RTC, my angels Ashton Brianna Gant and Gabrielle Annette Gant were born in Lake Forest, Ill on December 5th, 1997. Ashton Brianna was a name Stacey had already picked out years ago, and we knew we would name her that. When we heard we were having twins, we struggled to find a name for the second girl. A name is forever, and we were not good with names at all. We had named our cat "Kitty." I know, original right? We finally settled on Gabrielle Annette. Ashton came first with a gasp and a cry, and Gabby was born two minutes later. At first, I saw her foot sticking out like it was testing the water of the world, and it pulled back in like it had touched Lake Michigan in the winter. The doctor said she was backwards and needed to be turned around. No one panicked, and the doctor began to try to move her around but could not do it. So, she hooked two fingers on Gabby's hips and pulled her out butt first. Gabby was born mooning everyone in the room and I still laugh about that to this day.

Great Lakes would require my full attention and round-the-clock dedication, and I was starting to see the strain it was putting on my family. Things were further unraveling, and we masked it with busyness and travel. Stacey was caring for the girls, and I was making myself available the best I could—or was I?

After a highly successful four-year tour as a division commander, I had also attended the Naval Leadership School in Great Lakes, and, in the last two years, taught the new RDC's how to do their jobs. I had been hand selected out of all the staff on base to be advanced to the paygrade of Damage Controlman First Class, which was a tremendous honor to be selected for based on the high caliber of people I was stationed with. When I left there, I was given my choice of orders, and, due to the strenuous level of hours involved in my job, I chose to go to Pre-Comm unit later to be known as USS *McCampbell* DDG 85.

A pre-comm or pre-commission is a ship that has not been built yet. It was going to be built in

Bath, Maine, at Bath Iron Works (BIW). Each place I was stationed, I was put to the test at different levels and different environments. This would be no different. I had never helped start a command, but I had experience and the ability to organize a ship to change homeports to Guam. As a division commander, I had the leadership ability to get men to work as a team. I had construction ability to understand plans, building procedures, metal working, and welding. How hard could this be? It seemed like everything I had done in life was bringing me to this point.

The best part of the new job was that we would be moving to San Diego, CA. I would be attending Navy schools there that would last for over a year and a half. What an awesome way to get some time off with the family. I could go to class until noon and spend time with the family the other half the day. Finally, I would get some time to mend the relational cracks that had formed in my marriage. Don't misunderstand me, we had some good times, had seen a lot of places, and done some fun stuff, but it was no match for consistent family time. Providing essentials and money was one thing, but I was now understanding that I was great at what I did but had no idea how to be a husband or a father. I was finally ready to start making amends with my family.

We drove our van loaded with stuff, pulling the Saturn behind us from Chicago to San Diego.

It was a pretty good trip, the Rocky Mountains were awesome, Las Vegas was bright, and the Mohave Desert was a wild stretch. We arrived at our new place and stayed at the Navy Lodge until we moved into our apartment in Tierrasanta. We got settled in and realized how small the 800-sqft. apartment was with two adults and two toddlers, but we would manage. Plus, with the cost of rent in San Diego, it was all we could afford.

The day finally came, and I would receive my school schedule. I had reported to Naval Station San Diego's Command office and went to personnel to get my orders and schedule for the next year and a half. Navy schools were always easy and, as everyone knows, pretty skate. "Skate" was another Navy term for easy, just slowly skating around with ease. Easy hours and home early every day, nothing really taxing. All you really had to do was show up.

When I asked for my school schedule, the PN2 at the personnel office reviewed the list and said, "DC1, you don't get a class schedule, you have an Ord-mod."

The blood quickly drained from my face as he said those words, Ord-mod. That meant an orders modification. My first thought was to quickly reach out and choke him until he passed out, thinking no one would notice, but that's not allowed, or at least legal, even in today's Navy. He informed me that the HT1 in Maine had got a DUI and was being relieved of his position.

The personnel office informed me that in two weeks I was to fly to Bath, Maine to replace the HT1 on the ship. No schools, no break, no family time, nothing! There I was again. On the ride home, I thought of a way I had to tell Stacey again that the plans had changed, and I would be moving to the opposite corner of the US. You literally could not move farther away from each other on the lower 48 states.

I asked the command if I could move my family there with me and was told I could, but I would have to pay for it all and the rent of our house. Sure, let us move again, but now from Sunny California to the frozen state of Maine. Weighing my options, we decided I would go to Maine alone for the next year and a half. I believe now that this was the final nail that was put in the marriage coffin. The lack of time and attention for the last ten years was starting to take its toll. My relentless pursuit to be the best for me and those around me was robbing me of what mattered the most, my wife and my kids.

I packed some things, and Stacey and the girls took me to the airport. We said our goodbyes and took a picture together. Leaving that day, I knew things would never be the same between us. The gap was getting wider and wider. I felt like I was missing this opportunity to make things right. What else could I do? Quit? It had crossed my mind once or twice. We assured each other that I would come visit as much as I could and call often. We remained married, but I was again at work too much and now living hundreds of miles away.

The flight was late, and I arrived in Portland, Maine around 3:00AM. I was picked up and dropped off at the barracks at the Brunswick Naval Station in Brunswick, Maine. I was put with a roommate who was another first class, but he was on leave that week with his family. Alone in that dorm room, I lay there, still tired, but unable to sleep. With the sun coming up, I was again in a completely different environment. The sense of dread was overwhelming. I felt like the end was near. I tossed around for a few hours, then decided to watch TV to battle the jet lag. After turning to ESPN for a few minutes I channel surfed just long enough to stop and see the second plane hit the World Trade Center in New York City. The date was Sep 11th, 2001.

Lord, thank you for helping me see the bigger picture of the world you created and helping me to see my place in it. Even with the endless ups and downs in life, you help me see that there is so much more going on behind the scenes. You help me see that each event is an opportunity to learn and grow through those trials. Thank you for pushing me. Thank you for the trials and your loving hand as I stumble.

A LIFETIME OF PREPARATION

Chapter 4

WHAT DOESN'T KILL YOU, ONLY MAKES YOU STRONGER.

Where were you when the world stopped turnin'
That September day?
Were you in the yard with your wife and children
Or workin' on some stage in L.A.?
Did you stand there in shock at the sight of that black
smoke
Risin' against that blue sky?
Did you shout out in anger, in fear for your neighbor
Or did you just sit down and cry?

-Alan Jackson

AS ALAN JACKSON ONCE SANG, where were you when the world stopped turnin' that September day? Each person old enough remembers where they were on the eleventh day of September 2001. My first morning at my new duty station at Naval Air station Brunswick, Maine started out on lock down and continued for a solid week, no one in or out. The only people I had contact with was the few others in the dorm rooms around me. The first two days, I ate some of the food my roommate had stored up, Ramen noodles and canned soup, using a small microwave. A small group got together, and we started to walk to the Shaw's grocery store located outside the front gate. It was decided that we needed to gather supplies until the head of command figured out the security situation. We gathered the money we had on us and went to get the essentials which turned out to be beer, steaks, and potatoes.

We did what would come naturally and grilled out for the next four days until someone came. The first person that arrived was a First-Class Petty Officer who, once he introduced himself, I realized was the guy I was replacing who got the DUI. This was the guy who destroyed my plans and diverted me here. My first thought was to verbally kill him right there where he stood, but his lackadaisical attitude over how he had altered my life had me scratching my head.

I spent my entire year and a half in Maine living mostly out of hotel rooms, and because I had so much time off, I was working a second job at a movie store across the street called The Movie Gallery. I liked the movie store, and I got to take home all the movies I wanted for free.

A ship being built was an awesome sight to see, but it was kind of boring too. The highlights of our evenings would be getting folding chairs, drinking beer, and sitting across the street from the shipyard, watch them weld ship sections together. It reminded me of the winters in Sasebo, Japan, sitting outside the open door of the foundry. There we had drunk hot canned coffee from the vending machines and watched them pour red hot molten metal into forms to make various parts for ships. You could feel the heat flowing out the huge open garage doors and would often have to shield your eyes from the bright glow of the molten metal being poured. I always marveled at the fact that, several times a day, the Japanese would sound a horn, and the workers would stop and do exercises right where they were to remain flexible. We could learn something from that as a society.

In Maine, when you put that many sailors in one place with nothing to do, trouble is bound to happen. One winter night, the temperature was in the lower twenties and snowing, as I crossed the highway from my movie rental job to the hotel I was living in, I saw a fire truck across from my hotel. Someone had been cooking out in their room with the window open, and smoke billowed out onto the cold street. In the bathroom, the fire department found a rice cooker going, baked potatoes in the microwave, a hot plate cooking peppers and onions in a pan, and a pot of boiling water for the lobsters that were crawling around in the bathtub. The smoke from the peppers and onions cooking on the hotplate had set off the smoke alarm. The room was my friend's, and I had been on my way to that very cookout.

I stood outside in the snow by the fire truck and pretended I had no idea what had happened. The manager of the hotel was a retired master chief, and we had a little more leniency with him. After a few beers in the hotel bar, all was forgiven and forgotten. Besides he was making thousands a month by renting all his rooms out to the Navy.

When the ship was completed, we sailed from the icy waters of the Kennebec River south, past Florida and through the Panama Canal to San Diego, CA. Our official commissioning ceremony was scheduled to be in San Francisco later that year. I was home, and we completed numerous deployments to South America, usually for counter narcotics operations.

During my last year in San Diego, I received the news that every career sailor looks for. I was selected for the next paygrade of E7; I would be a Chief Petty Officer. This is the level each sailor strives for, to be accepted by his peers and recognized for his efforts. It didn't matter how many medals I had earned or commendations I was given. I had finally arrived!

All the work had paid off. I was at the pinnacle of my career, but my personal, spiritual life and marriage was in shambles. I was damage controlman by trade, but I could not control the damage in my own relationships.

During my indoctrination process for Chief, I had a friend in the Chief's Mess by the name of ENC (SW) Bruce "Goose" Farris. Goose was the kind of guy, who, when I'd come in from drinking, would be sitting in the Chief's Mess dining area with his Bible in front of him, reading. I would come in drunk sometimes and get a drink or eat cereal before going to my bunk. We would talk, and he would share scripture into the late hours, just like Mrs. Cook had done back in Sumter after the late band practices.

During our opening night for initiation into the Chief's Mess, Goose and some of the other CPO's met for the night's events at the beach in San Diego. For the next twelve hours, I was going to go through my right of passage to be a Chief. It was dark, and I had no idea what was about to happen to me. As we stood around in a circle on that beach in San Diego, with the sounds of the crashing waves around us, Goose looked at me and said, "Steve, would you lead us in prayer before we start?"

Prayer? Really? Me? Umm, okay! Throughout my entire life, I always kind of knew Jesus, and He absolutely knew me. But I never really took it seriously. Like my marriage, I had placed my spiritual walk in the background, always telling myself there was time. Now here I was on the pinnacle of my career, and Goose taught me that no matter what is going on, there is always time to talk to God. The night was one for the record books, and will not be talked about here, but I left the next day, twelve hours later, with the definition of the brotherhood of the Chief's Mess etched in my heart and God on my mind. My two worlds were on a collision course.

My career was very successful, and my family went on to move to Mayport Naval station in Jacksonville, FL. At the Naval Training Center, I taught leadership school, wrote curriculum for the school, and taught hundreds of men and women what it's like to be a leader. Over the next three years, I got more time off and time with my family. I loved to teach people and help them unlock their potential. I had done it all my career; whether it was training commands or teaching firefighting on the ships, leadership was in my blood. The way I showed people I cared was by giving them the knowledge and ability to do something better.

Old habits die hard, because that same drive to lead and teach men pushed me to volunteer to serve in Iraq with an Individual Augment (IA) Detail. The Navy personnel worked alongside Army Personnel in various operations in the frontlines of the battle on Terrorism. IA's filled the gap that combat trained solders lacked. I attended the training in Fort McGregor, New Mexico with some of the finest soldiers and sailors in the field. And on top of that, we got to train on all kinds of weapons and vehicles.

I remained in Mayport and was transferred to my last ship, The USS *Samuel B. Roberts* FFG 58. I was the damage control chief onboard, the ship's fire marshal, and the leader of the damage control training team. I was also responsible for the Repair Division, which conducted all things maintenance on all parts of the ship. I was still able to live in Mayport and get more time at home between deployments. The Sammy "B" was the tightest team I had ever worked with. That tour was the best of my career.

(Photo taken from the author)
Back row middle with the mustache

The essence of teamwork was revealed to me while on deployment off the west coast of Africa. For the last two months, we had been monitoring shipping traffic fifty miles off the coast of Lagos, Nigeria. The choice currency used by terrorists today is drugs and human trafficking, in which West Africa was a hotbed of activity.

By my own merit, I had risen to the rank of Chief Petty Officer in the field of engineering. I still believed that I held the key to my own success through hard work and self-motivation. I have always been self-driven and qualified for anything I could get my hands on, from engineering systems to small arms weapons.

When it came to firefighting and damage control, teamwork was essential. We ate, slept, worked, and often drank together and were always around each other. We trained together as a team until we knew each person's moves before they did. In a causality situation, we needed to react by instinct, not verbal communication, because engine rooms were loud enough to drown out even the loudest commands. After being a member of this team, I was not used to working with people I did not know.

One night, we received intelligence that a go-fast in the area was making a break from the coastal waters to run drugs to a larger ship out on the open ocean. A go-fast is a small open hulled boat, usually large enough to accommodate five grown men and operate under the radar by posing as a fishing vessel. These small crafts are usually outfitted with one 125-horsepower outboard motor which would suffice for a fishing boat of its size. But when used to run drugs, they would mount up to three 200-HP motors, hence the term "go-fast." The runners would overload these boats with motors and kilos of cocaine that filled the boat so high, they would be walking on kilos like it was the floor itself. With that kind of power, a go-fast could outrun a full-size frigate, but they still could never outrun a helicopter.

We quickly went to the flight quarters and launched the helicopter. The helicopter's job was to catch up with the go-fast and, with a trained sharpshooter, shoot out the engines.

Late that evening, I received a call that the captain would like to speak to me on the bridge. Upon arriving, the captain motioned me over to brief me on the current situation. The Bridge is the command center of the ship and a very busy place. I could barely hear him over the commotion, so we stepped outside to hear him better. Once outside, we were now surrounded by the blackness of the open sea. The dark, tranquil vastness of the sea normally seemed so peaceful to sailors, but that same darkness could bring swift terror at the thought of floating in it alone. The weather deck was always my favorite place to be while underway, with the wind in my face, the smell of salt in the air, and the expanse that is the ocean. At night, the stars could be seen from horizon to horizon, like being inside the world's largest planetarium.

The Captain explained to me, "We just received word that the helicopter has shot out some of the engines, and the go-fast is at a stop. The crew is attempting to dump the cocaine overboard."

"Aye, sir," I replied. "What can I do to help?"

The captain steadied himself against the heavy waves slapping the ship by gripping the starboard rail. "Chief, I need to recover the small craft, the men, and the drugs that are in and out of the water. We don't have time to wait for sunrise, so we'll have to do it in the dark."

I thought about the logistics of pulling off an operation of this magnitude and instantly began to formulate a plan.

The captain interrupted me mid-thought. "We are also under a time crunch because the boat is sinking. You are the most qualified to do the repairs and can carry a tactical weapon."

I was now leaning on the starboard rail, but not because of the heavy seas, but the gravity of the situation.

"I will do my best, sir," I replied, and with an encouraging nod of his head, he turned and walked away.

I proceeded to the armory to be issued a holstered 9MM pistol and a floatation vest, and, in route to the loading area, I grabbed my tool bag.

The boarding team got ready and was loading into the Ridged Hull Inflatable Boat (RHIB). The RHIB had one engine and could hold around six people. I greeted the team leader and introduced myself to the rest of the team. He introduced the team members and briefed us on what to expect.

"Because of the hole in the go-fast, they sent Chief Gant to assess the situation," the team leader said. "To see if he can plug the leak or get the remaining motors running before we take on too much water."

I had never been in this type of situation before, much less been trained for it. I was completely out of my element. I had learned to depend on teammates that I knew, but I knew none of these men. I always planned for the seen but never the unforeseen, and I would have to be as flexible as Gumby on this mission.

It's one thing to see a small craft like a go-fast from the deck of a big Navy ship, but once we were at sea level, every wave was like a wall. We began the slow ride to locate the hostiles. The sound of the wind and waves made it difficult to hear one another already. We would rise about twenty feet on one wave, then, just as we would reach the peak, we'd zoom down the other side just to do it all over again. It was like a roller coaster except for two details: no one would've been shooting at us on a roller coaster, and on this ride, no one was laughing. My left hand had a white-knuckled grip on a piece of rope tied to the hull, and I was not about to let go. My right hand was on the grip of the 9MM Beretta on my hip. I had long ago earned my sea legs, and I had not felt this unsteady on my feet since my first day on a ship fifteen years ago.

Because of their high vantage point and the use of radar, the Bridge radio operator informed us how close we were to the hostiles. We drove and drove, up and down; it felt like we were going in circles. I questioned the coxswain's ability to navigate the craft, then settled in on the fact that I could do no better and would have to trust him. We could not see the hostiles from our low vantage point against the high waves.

Then the radio from the ship began shouting, "They're right in front of you! They are right there!"

We could hear them yelling, but still saw nothing in the darkness. Moments later, we came over the next big wave and almost landed right on top of the go-fast. We drew our weapons, but, to our surprise, they already had their hands up and gave little resistance. With terrified looks on their faces, they let us board.

After we rounded up the prisoners, I assessed the situation. A bullet from the sharpshooter on the helicopter had passed through the engine block and gone through the bottom of the hull. Just a small bullet hole, but it was still taking on water, nonetheless. Twelve men all working on a boat meant for five was going to be tight. We'd have to learn to work together as a team quickly.

Standing in shin-deep water, I informed the team lead that we had about thirty minutes before the water would fill the boat, and with this number of people onboard and the action of the waves, it might be sooner.

The team leader looked me straight-faced and replied, "Well, Chief, it looks like we're going to be swimming because it's going to take at least an hour to process this stuff."

I knew I had to improvise, so with my gun trained on a prisoner, I saw a bucket floating and started to bail as the team secured the prisoners in restraints.

My job was simple, just keep the boat afloat for as long as I could. I had to laugh to myself at this situation. Here I had millions of dollars in the latest equipment onboard a state-of-the-art war vessel. I had years of training at my disposal, only to realize that sometimes all you need is the ability to adapt and a two-dollar bucket.

While I was bailing, my flashlight shone on the water in the boat, and something struck me as out of place. There seemed to be the normal mixture of fuel and oil, but there was also another substance on the surface of the water. It looked a lot like blood. I informed the team, and upon further inspection, we uncovered the tarp of drugs and found a man on the forward part of the craft, face down in a pool of blood.

The radio crackled to the Bridge. "We have one hostile down. He appears to have been shot, still breathing."

After stabilizing him, we checked him from head to toe to find the source of the bleeding. We found that he had been hit in the right buttock. Again, having to adjust on the fly, one man treated the causality by keeping pressure on the wound. I continued to bail water, while the others unloaded all the men and cargo.

We got everyone back onboard and started to debrief the captain. It was concluded that the man who had been shot had been sitting at the back of the boat when the helicopter fired at it. The bullet passed through the engine block. Shrapnel from the engine, not the bullet, had hit him. If a sharpshooter bullet had struck him directly, there would've been no butt left to deal with.

Overall, I did not know my new team, nor did they know me, but, using patience and flexibility, the team was successful. It took us ten trips and five hours to unload everything and everyone. The team arrested five drug runners, treated one personal causality, secured all the evidence, and seized 200 kilos of cocaine. It was the largest drug bust we had on deployment to date. What I would take away from this is being successful, self-driven, and well trained would only take me so far, but being part of a fluid team is being part of something greater and much more rewarding for both me and the country.

(Photo taken from the author)
Trying to keep the go-fast from sinking. You can see the hole and the water coming in. The boat was not big, but the ocean at night is.

WEIGHED, MEASURED, AND FOUND WANTING

I was at the top of my game, the pinnacle of my profession. I had my identity, but life was not all it seemed to be. It was during this same time that the years of neglect in my marriage began to show. Even though I was home and able to spend more time with my family, too much damage had been done, and one day, Stacey took the girls and moved out. Sure, I had set the professional bar high and attained it. I had fulfilled my dream. But, at the same time, I was also divorced, alone, and went from one failed relationship to another. My days were highlighted by drinking in my garage and waiting for my week of visitation with my girls.

Instead of having them walk the six blocks from the school bus stop to their mom's house after school, I would go to the bus stop, so I could drive them the few blocks home just to get a few more minutes with them. Time was very important, and it never seemed like I had enough. During my career, I had to go on many deployments and operations, most of them six months long. I succeeded as the provider and got them anything they ever needed. But I now understood that it was not the provision that mattered, it was the time.

Stacey, my wife of sixteen years, had left me, and I spent the next three and a half years going through a divorce and moving from one train wreck of a relationship to another. I seemed to focus in on certain types of women, ones that were always in a troubled relationship already, who I could save by swooping in. Then, like a couple of addicts, we would cling on to one another, until, in the end we ultimately self-destructed.

One night, it all came to a head when some friends and I had gone to watch football at a sports bar in Jacksonville. We invited some people from the bar back to my house for a cookout, hot tub, and drinks. I liked to entertain people and have fun, and I considered myself a pretty good host. As I was mixing drinks at the bar outside and watching everyone have a good time, a girl dropped a drink into the hot tub and her reply as she laughed was, "It's no big deal, it will be fine." The next minute, some guy broke a glass in my kitchen, and I heard them all laughing.

As I stood there and looked around, I realized that I only knew one person there out of fifteen people, and that was my girlfriend. I put down the glass, turned down the music and told everyone to get out of my house. Shortly after that, I broke up with that girlfriend. I realized that all the people around me were sucking the life out of me. Everything I had come to depend on was gone. Everything I had put my faith in was collapsing around me. I had a house full of stuff, a garage full of music equipment, a bachelor pad that would make most men jealous, more friends that I needed, but I was completely alone and isolated.

I had grown up with the name of Jesus surrounding me, but I never really knew who He was to me. I had encounter after encounter with Him, through people God had put in my path, but I had continued my own way. As I mentioned before, it would take the direct intervention of an angel to get my attention, and like Peter, get me on my knees. My angels would be Ashton and Gabby.

My ex-wife Stacey, her new boyfriend Doug, and I had remained friends, and they even lived across the street from me for a few years. That way, the girls could come and go to each house with ease. On October fourth, 2010, we had all gone to Kernan Blvd. Baptist Church in Jacksonville to watch a Christian group of strong men perform. These men broke baseball bats, tore phone books, broke wood blocks, and did other stuff strong men do. They also witnessed to the audience about their lives and how God was involved in it. During the middle of the show, the man on stage began talking about being saved.

Now Gabby and Ashton had gone to Word of Life Camp just weeks before this and had given their lives to Jesus and got baptized. We were so proud of them. As the man stood on stage and talked about being saved, Gabby turned to me and said, "Daddy, do you remember when you were saved?"

I thought about my past, growing up in the church, about Mike Warnke and being baptized as a baby. I replied to Gabby, "No, honey, I can't remember the exact day really, but I do remember when..."

As soon as I said that, the man on stage says "If you don't remember the day, there's a good chance that you were not, because it's a day you won't forget."

It was like three people talking as one. I looked at Gabby and Ashton, and for the first time, I felt ashamed and alive at the same time. I saw how much I had let them down, how much I had failed them as a spiritually leading father. Their faces were so bright and smiling, and I knew that God was using them to get a message to me. When they asked for children to come forward to give their lives to Jesus that night, they were to bring their parents with them. I got up and asked Gabby to come with me, to be a part of it. It would be a day I would always remember, the day that my twelve-year-old daughter would lead me home again. I was ready for a change, ready to be who God wanted me to be. Ready for my life to get better. Ready to submit myself to Him completely. I was finally on my knees in the boat.

As new believers, we are excited, electric with the Holy Spirit, like children again. In Matthew's Gospel, Jesus is baptized and has the approval of his Father in Heaven, the Holy Spirit come down on Him like a dove. In the very next verse, Jesus is led into the wilderness by the Spirit to be tempted of the devil. We can take comfort in the fact that the Spirit led Him there but look at the order in which it happens. The high point in any new believer's life is the repenting of our sin, letting go of the weight, accepting the Holy Spirit, and rejoicing in our new life. Jesus' example shows us that it's the very point the devil will attack when we are most vulnerable. On the fortieth day of His fast, at His weakest moment,

Satan will attack. Satan will try to push us over before we can get our spiritual roots deep enough. Even Jesus faced temptation, so why should not I expect the same? Trials were about to come, and I was going to let the Spirit led me the best I could. My time of temptation in the wilderness would begin immediately. The devil was waiting for me in the parking lot.

On the drive home, my mind raced with the thoughts of what would I tell the people on the ship. My fellow Chief Petty Officers? Could I tell them? Was I even worthy enough to make such a statement? I began to sweat bullets and worried the whole way home. When I got to my house that night, my friend, and roommate Jason was there, and we went out back to smoke a cigarette. We chatted and talked about little stuff. I thought to myself, "There's no way I can tell people this." Everyone knows me as the most profane, vulgar person. But I needed to start now.

I turned to Jason and said, "I got saved tonight," and waited for the hammer to fall.

"Wow!" He replied. "That's awesome! Good for you."

That was not too hard to do, and it was a good start. I walked into the Chiefs' Mess the next morning, stood in front of the 5 guys eating breakfast, and said, "I got saved last night, and I don't care what you think about it."

A few answered, "Cool" and "That's nice." No fanfare, but no criticism either. From that day on,

I would be a new Steve, a new man in God. This was a great first step, and it seemed that the spirt was leading me in baby steps. I figured I was through the hard part, but I could never have been more wrong.

Soon after this, I began suffering from back pain that caused a shooting sensation down my left leg. Finally, I went to get it looked at by a specialist. They said I had a pinched nerve in my back, and the MRI showed I would need surgery very soon. I put in for time off for the surgery; I would be down for two weeks to a month at least. Not the way I wanted to spend my final few months in the Navy. The plan was I would get the surgery done, I would go back to the ship after recovery, check out of the command, and set up the final few details for my retirement ceremony. My plan was to retire and start my own home repair business and manage rental properties. It seemed like the most logical thing.

As I prepared for the surgery, I was a little nervous but ready to end the pain. The doctor also informed me that heavy lifting would be a no for at least a year, and I was a little concerned with having to take a year off. The procedure went surprisingly well, they shaved a little off a bulging disk, but I would have to be off my feet for a while. It was one of the hardest things I ever had to do. It was painful to move around, but I would manage okay. They gave me a walker to use and a raised toilet seat. I thought, "Are you kidding? What am I, a hundred years old?"

I would soon find out that every inch of movement was like a mile. I was laid up for weeks, recovering at my house. As the days started to pass, the only people that came to see me, besides the home care nurse who would come by to check my sutures, was my ex-wife Stacey and my girls. No one from the Navy stopped by no one even called me, not one of them called to see if I was even alive. Here was my wilderness, my alone time.

As I lay there, I thought about how much I had sacrificed for the Navy and what I had done. It was a lot of time to think and reflect on what I had been doing. I was a captive audience of one for God to talk to me, and we had a lot of catching up to do. Who had I been working for all those years? I had been chasing the American dream and caught it, only to be left wanting more. I realized that, although I had been successful, I had done it for all the wrong reasons. Why had I done it? For me? For my wife? For the girls? Had all this time been wasted? I had kept myself so busy that I had no time to listen to God at all. I had filled my life with being so busy that I had pushed God out of my mind.

When people are hurting and lost in life, most will fill the void with drugs, drinking, hobbies, and work. Yes, work is a drug, and we can abuse it daily. In fact, I believe it destroys more families than any other substance. I am not saying do not go to work, but ask yourself what are you working for? Like alcohol, if not controlled or used in moderation, it will destroy lives and tear apart families. Like a good pain medication, it can take the edge off of the recovery of a surgery, but if not controlled, will take you over the edge of addiction and destroy thousands of lives. Work can be the gateway drug to things like infidelity, alcoholism, and other means to an end.

As men, we will sometimes cover our inability to communicate with our wives and children by working. Then all it takes is a woman to show us a little attention at work, and we will be off the path towards infidelity. We immerse ourselves in anything to avoid the realism of real life, and it becomes our escape. Keeping myself busy had been my way of escaping my reality.

During my recovery, God finally got my attention. It was not that He had left me or stopped talking to me. It all came down to the fact that He had been talking to me, I just wasn't listening. Lying on that bed, recovering from my surgery, I was finally listening. He has a funny way of getting our attention. As I laid there alone, all I could do was listen.

When I finally returned to the ship, I was using a cane and limping from the surgery. When I got onboard, they asked me "Hey, Chief, what happened to you? What did you do to yourself? Where have you been?"

I told them I had back surgery and had been recovering for almost a month. The shocking thing was, no one really seemed to know that I was gone. I had no idea what to say. For once in my life, I was speechless. I got my stuff from my sleeping quarters, had someone carry it to my car, and for my last thirty days, I literally never went back to work, and no one ever called.

The next time I heard from the Navy was when they sent me my end-of-tour award in the mail over six months after my time was officially done. My parents, a few months later, gave me a plaque to commemorate my career in the Navy and never really knew what had happened. Do not misunderstand me at all, I love the Navy, I love the men and women I served with. Some of the greatest memories I had were from those twenty years. The Chief's Mess are the brothers I will never forget. The problem was that I had been leaning on the Navy for so long and depended on them for everything. I had given them everything and really believed that my identity in the Navy would carry me throughout my life. I always thought, "How can the Navy survive without me?" Well, they will, and they did. It was like God saying, "So the Navy is your crutch? You want to lean on them?" And in a flash, it was all gone.

As I struggled a little with this thought, I knew I would have to make a huge change. My back was pretty much shot, and God had taken the Navy crutch I leaned on. I questioned how I could live off of half of what I used to make? What would I do for money? With my back condition, everything changed. Physical labor was out of the question for at least a year, and physical labor was all I knew. One thing gave me comfort during this season. Because of my back injury, once I retired, I knew I'd get disability through the Veterans Administration (VA) to make up for some of the financial loss I had. Through the VA, I could also apply to be trained for a new line of work, something less physical. Maybe I could be a teacher like Mr. Oates at the Career Center in Sumter? A Supervisor? The possibilities were endless.

The Navy had disappointed me and moved on without me, and that was hard for me to get past. I was injured from my service, but I tried not to worry because I knew the VA would help me financially pick up where the Navy dropped me off. Through the VA, I could count on financial help for my injury and retraining for a job. I never realized how right I was. The VA took up right where the Navy left off. 100% disappointed.

Lord, Through the highest of highs and the lowest of lows, you are there. That even when it seems like I am in my deepest despair, you show that your grace is sufficient. Help me to worship you on the mountain tops and in the valleys of life with equal enthusiasm.

Chapter 5

OUT OF THE FRYING PAN AND INTO ANOTHER FRYING PAN

I love the recklessness of faith. First you leap, then you grow wings.
—William Sloane Coffin

AS STATED BEFORE, I know God's timing is never off. The mistake we make is putting God on our clock and have Him play by our rules. We must understand that He is bigger than us and beyond our comprehension. Pride is what makes us attempt to pull God down to our level and force Him into a neat little package we designed for Him. This thought process causes the most disfunction between man and his Creator.

2 PETER 3:9

The Lord is not slow to fulfill his promise as some count slowness, but is patient toward you, not wishing that any should perish, but that all should reach repentance.

Just because I am a believer, does not mean life will be perfect. Change can always be viewed as scary. Trust is the process of transitioning from one major life event to another. It can also bring on a renewing of yourself, a fresh start, a moment when you can hit the reset button.

As I was approaching the end of a twenty-year career in the US Navy, I could sit back and evaluate everything I had done, all my accomplishments and milestones. I thought back on the friendships and family bonds that had been formed. Even though God had removed my Navy crutch I leaned on, I had the VA to pull me through. My back injury would keep me out for at least a year. Living on half pay, I would be able to receive disability from the VA and they could teach me a new, less physical trade.

Because of the divorce, Stacey was entitled to fifty percent of my fifty percent. I knew I could not work and now had to live on a quarter of what I used to. I called the VA and asked them how long it would take to complete my disability claim and when I could start to re-train for a new job. They informed me that it would take an estimated one and a half years to complete the paperwork and review my case. The retraining could not be scheduled until I got that approval for disability after that one and a half years of waiting. The month I retired; it was all coming at me at once. God had taken the Navy from me, and now He took the VA crutch away. I felt as if I was caught in the perfect storm of life. Everything that could go wrong was happening and at the worst times. I wondered, "Why, God, are you punishing me now?" It's a question many people will ask themselves and God. I had seen the error of my ways, I got on my knees in the boat of my life, repented, and asked for forgiveness. Why was all this happening to me now? After all, I was a believer and knew God would provide for me.

People believe that once you are saved, your life will be perfect, and nothing can go wrong. I referred to Jesus and His time in the wilderness. I was in my wilderness again, and this question took a while to pray as I waited for Him, but at least I was praying and waiting. I was finally taking a step in the right direction and was depending on Him.

When we are not in tune to God's will, we think we have "bad luck" and are being punished for doing wrong. We ask, "God, why are you punishing me?" But when you seek God's will and plan, it is no longer called "bad luck" or "punishment," it is called receiving directions. When we submit ourselves to His will, resistance in our lives is minimal, because God paves the way and opens doors. When things seem to be going wrong, I now look to God for a new direction He has laid out. I had been leaning on all the wrong things, and now that I was open to His "direction," I was all ears and ready to learn. Patience was starting to pay off, and I received my answer in the most unlikely ways. Stacy had decided to go against her lawyer, and she allowed me to keep my whole retirement.

Leaving the Navy, I was now entitled to get 50% of what I used to make. Even on fifty percent pay, financially I was a train wreck and needed something to pay the bills. I thought and prayed that something would come. I decided the only thing I could do was go back to work and pray for the best. It was early for my back recovery to start working again, but my savings would only take me so far, and it was going fast. I purchased a trailer and tools on credit and started to build my home repair business from the ground up.

Using everything I knew and all the credit I had, I started my business, and it seemed to be going well. My focus was on spiritual growth, Ashton and Gabby, and work in that order. Spiritual growth and God always came first, because when it did, everything else seemed right with my girls and work. I understood that instead of focusing on all the problems in life, I just needed to focus on God, and everything else would fall into place. I had to learn to do without and get creative. Walking with Him daily was like baby steps. I had to get back my childlike faith. The first thing I needed to do was to stop overthinking things and just follow. I took every minute I could get to be around the girls. I wanted to end jobs early just to be at the bus stop, see them get off the bus, and drive them home. Even after the divorce, Stacey and I remained friends, and her boyfriend Doug Powell, the girls, and I all attended East Pointe Church.

One day, I was looking for more work, and my neighbor Darla gave me the number of a church friend who attended Celebration Church with her. Darla had gone on a mission trip with this girl and knew she needed some work done on her house. Her name was Gina DeBoer. I went to check on the job and met Gina. I was working with Stacy's boyfriend Doug, and it took a few days for us to finish the job at Gina's house. When I went by her house to get paid, she said she didn't have much time to talk because she was on her way to a meeting for a mission trip she was going on to Africa. I said I had been to Africa a few times for different reasons but liked it there. She said she was going to Zimbabwe on a medical mission's trip. After she left, I thought about her for a few days and could not get her off my mind. I wanted to ask her out for coffee or something, but she was nine years younger than me, and dating was the last thing on my mind. I thought, if I asked her out, she may've thought I was some creepy old man and pepper spray me or something. I had sworn off dating seven months before and was very serious about following God's direction. I was ready to be a monk or to join the priesthood. I decided to just let it go and move on with my life. I was already having enough challenges on my own and was doing all I could to just let God walk before me. God was no longer my co-pilot; He was my pilot.

About four weeks later, I received a text from Darla, and she told me that Gina, the girl I did the work for, had just been diagnosed with a brain aneurism and needed us all to pray for her. A brain aneurism is a weak artery wall in the brain, which creates a bubble of blood that could burst, and if this happens, a person can die. I started to text those I knew to join us in prayer for Gina. I also texted her to let her know we were all praying for her and she had support.

After that day, I continued to text her and ask for updates on her condition. I was not sure if it was welcomed or not, but I felt a draw to her and wanted to be part of her prayer group. She responded to my text and didn't block me, change her number, or file for a restraining order, so things were going well. I liked her and had wanted to ask her out but lost my nerve. I have learned to always allow God to lead me in the direction He wants. After a few weeks, I finally asked her out to the movies, just to get to know each other. To this day, neither of us are sure if it was an actual date or not. I had tickets to see the movie *Soul Surfer* about the life of Bethany Hamilton. I picked Gina up in my truck and had my daughters Ashton, Gabrielle, my neighbor Darla, and her boyfriend's son Alex with me. I cannot imagine what she was thinking. I was too old to play games, and I guess I was just laying it all out there and letting her know that I was a forty-year-old, divorced father of two beautiful twin teenage girls. I had nothing to hide, so there I was. It must have gone well because there was no pepper spray, no mace, nothing. In fact, I quickly followed up with a second date. The next day, Gina went shoe shopping with the girls and me. Guys, if you want to get to know a girl, take her shoe shopping.

As the day approached for her aneurism surgery, we prayed fervently and prepared ourselves. I wondered if this was another test from God. It seemed He had taken so much away, and my new-found faith was being tested daily. Was I following His direction? Was I on the path He chose for me? I wondered if I was still trying to open a closed door. Would He bring Gina into my life just to take her away? During this time, it was different. It was not fear that consumed me but wonder. I eagerly looked forward to seeing what God was going to do now. I would have to sit, and yes, you guessed it... wait. There is another word for patience in the Bible, and that is longsuffering. Suffering for anything righteous makes it all worthwhile and all the sweeter.

1 PETER 4:12-13

[12] *Beloved, think it not strange concerning the fiery trial which is to try you, as though some strange thing happened unto you:*

[13] *But rejoice, inasmuch as ye are partakers of Christ's sufferings; that, when his glory shall be revealed, ye may be glad also with exceeding joy.*

Even if the trial is small, celebrate in the joy of your trust and faith that grows bigger. Through small victories, we are preparing for the bigger battles that will be fought and won.

After some prayer and thought, Gina had decided to go ahead and have the surgery to take care of the aneurism. Since we had known each other for only a few weeks, I did not go to the hospital, but her friend Jill went with her. I had her on speed dial and on my mind. The procedure was done by inserting a tube into the front of her hip and running it through to her brain. Before the procedure was to start the doctor said, "Let's run one more test before we start."

"What test?" Gina asked. She was never told of this test.

We were all surprised to hear this because this procedure was never mentioned before. It was called a cerebral angiogram. They would inject dye to locate the bulge, so they knew the exact location, size, and shape before the surgery. This was a final prep, just to make sure they knew where to work. They completed the test, and the doctor came in and informed Jill in the waiting room that they found nothing on the test. Gina could go home; she was healed. She would have to come back every five years.

Gina texted me to inform me of the good news that the aneurism was gone. We started to question whether it was just a mistake or if the doctor had missed something. It is strange how we witnessed a miracle and still started to question it being real. Sometimes we become so desensitized to the Holy Spirit, we think we can explain our way out of things. It was a genuine miracle from God and everyone involved celebrated. To God be the glory. God had told me Gina was here to stay and the relationship had His blessing. At least, that is the way I read it.

The things God does in people's lives are on such a large scale, larger than we will ever know. Most will categorize them as good and bad, but it is always God's plan. Nothing will ever happen causing God to say, "Well, I never saw that coming." He knows it all, nothing will surprise Him.

We started to ask ourselves, "Was this a test of faith for all involved? Will it change the life of someone we may never meet? Did he give her an aneurism, so I would get the nerve to ask her out?" Well, it worked, and a few months later I would ask her to marry me, and she would say "yes."

Gina had returned from her medical missions' trip to Zimbabwe, which had been very productive. I waited for her at the airport with flowers because she deserved them. By the end of the year, my business was going well. We were busy but not too busy. I married Gina on October 9th, 2011. A few months later the girls' mother, Stacey married Doug Powell. We all went to the wedding, and we remain friends to this day.

Our personal lives were coming together as well as our spiritual ones. Gina was working at TD Auto Finance, and I owned GP Discount Enterprises Home Repair and Property Rental. Things were really starting to fall into place.

In January 2012, I was out removing a door frame with a crowbar at one of the rental properties and the door frame won. My back announced that it had enough with a loud cracking sound and left me on the ground for twenty minutes catching my breath. That day, I started to realize that my body was rejecting the work that once came easy. I was once the strongest man around, but those days were over. I had done some real damage this time and would need rods inserted in the lower third of my back to form a cage to keep my lower spine together. The doctor told me this one would be a little more extensive; muscles and tissue would have to be moved around for the surgery and that would cause some pain after the surgery and a longer healing process. He told me that a Navy Seal had the same surgery and remained in pain for months. I was no Navy Seal, and I was not in any kind of shape for this.

During my first surgery, I had grown accustomed to Percocet and muscle relaxers. I remember being so afraid of getting hooked on them that time. When I got home after the first surgery, I told the nurse I really did not want to take them but would keep them by the bed just in case.

Rolling her eyes, she said, "Whatever you say Mr. Gant." She left me, and I lay down for a nap. I did not realize that full doses of morphine and anesthesia were still in my system, and I woke up like a bolt of lightning when they ran out. It felt like I had been kicked by a mule in my lower back, even simply breathing hurt. I curled up in the fetal position and grabbed the bottle, took a pill, and spilled water all over myself. I looked like a baby needing a bib. It is hard to drink water in the fetal position while trying not to breathe too deeply. The sight, now that I think about it, must have been hilarious.

From that first surgery, I was always very cautious about taking the meds at all. My brother David said, "You want to be careful taking them, because the next thing you know you're wearing flannel shirts, laying around the house watching *Days of Our Lives* and re-runs of *Big Brother,* and telling people everything's cool."

After the second surgery, the cage was installed in my back, and I seemed to be on my feet a little faster. Not as much pain, I just needed to move slower for a while. Recovery would take a while, but after about six months, I could get around relatively well. I did have to walk around with a big, wide back brace on, the kind that screams, "Look at me! I had back surgery!" One day, I was at the grocery store and saw a man in a wheelchair down one of the aisles. As I got in line, I ended up behind him.

He turned, noticed my brace, and said, "Oh, you had back surgery?"

"I did," I replied.

He pointed at his wheelchair. "Whatever you do, don't let them put that cage thing in your back, you see where that got me."

At that moment, the blood drained from my face, and all I could do was give him an awkward smile and halfhearted laugh. I thought about what made us different. Why was he in a wheelchair? Would I end up there? Surely not me, God would never allow that.

Six months later, I started to have some pains and a popping feeling in my back. I went for a follow up with the doctor, and he looked at my X-rays to tell me what was wrong. He explained to me that calcium and bone should be growing around the hardware and becoming one solid piece, but after six months of healing he informed me that it looked like I'd had surgery yesterday. Internally I had not healed at all; in fact, the popping feeling were the screws moving in and out of the bone in my spine. I would need another surgery, and soon, to install larger screws.

He asked me if I still smoked, and I said I did. I had been a smoker since I was around sixteen years old, and I was now forty-one. The doctor explained that a normal, healthy body would take one year to heal from this kind of surgery, but a smoker's body could take three years to get the same results.

The top surgeon in Jacksonville looked at me and said, "Steve, as your doctor and your friend, I'm telling you to quit smoking and quit smoking now. Do not misunderstand me, I'll keep working on you every six months. I could use the work and the money, but to tell you the truth, you are destroying yourself. Also, the work you do has to stop, and now."

It was like a bomb had gone off. Stop working? Quit smoking? I was stunned. I walked out to my truck, sat in the parking lot, and thought about my future. Like that day at Dillon

Ballpark in Sumter with that twelve-pack of beer, I was at a major crossroads in my life. I had quit smoking before at Great Lakes, but it did not last.

As I drove out of the parking lot of the hospital, I smoked a cigarette and thought about how I would proceed with this difficult decision. I simply prayed, "God, I need to quit smoking, and I need to do it now." After almost twenty-five years of smoking, I flipped that cigarette out the window and never looked back. Today to think about my smoking is almost like a dream. Like the devil trying to remind me of my past sins, I now get a yearly reminder from the VA in the form of a lung cancer scan to make sure my past has not caught up with me. Many people will attempt to quit addictions, but no patch, medicine, gum, or pill outdoes good old-fashioned willpower through the Holy Spirit. As I went into my third surgery to have bigger screws installed, I knew I was not going to end up in that wheelchair. I knew the recovery would go well. I knew my life was going to be better. God wasn't punishing me, He was directing me, blessing me out of fiery trials. Providing me with life direction through something that could have been considered bad luck before. I stopped cooking as much, and Gina started to cook healthy food for us all, and I took calcium to help the healing. We were taking better care of ourselves.

Now that my health was getting some much-needed attention, when it came to work, how would I make a living? I had to stop smoking and stop doing what I did best, which was heavy labor. After almost a year and a half, I was still waiting on the VA for a disability ruling on my back and the chance of retraining for a new career. That was at least another year away. How would we pay bills? Pay off all the debt? How could we survive on just retirement, and what would we do with our time?

We had been living the American dream for years and were drowning in debt. We owed an estimated $40,000 USD in student loans and credit cards. The question we had was, "How do we get ourselves out of the debt we are in?" God had the answer in a man named Dave Ramsey.

Gina had taken Dave Ramsey's course called Financial Peace University (FPU) two times before we met. Dave Ramsey is a man of God first and financial wizard second. He teaches you biblical things about tithing, paying off debt, and budgeting. We learned how we could live a happy, productive, debt free life and still do the things we wanted to. If you want something, you just save up for it, and it becomes much more rewarding when you achieve it. In 2012, on a twenty-four-hour drive to Gina's home state of Wisconsin from Jacksonville, we listened to all the Financial Peace University CDs together. We knew we could have better, debt free lives if we just applied it and focused our attention on doing it. As most FPU grads will tell you, it is hard to start, but once you get going, it's a habit. Around the same time the doctor had laid it out for me that the smoking had to go, we knew the debt also had to go.

The same as smoking, debt was a bad habit. No matter what financial course you take, book you read, budget spreadsheet you design, nothing beats good old-fashioned willpower from the Holy Spirit. When it comes to money, you can win the lottery and pay off your debt, but if you don't stop the money from leaking out of your budget, you will quickly be in debt again.

East Pointe Church sponsored the course, and through the grace of God, Gina and I graduated from the course. We took it on Sunday mornings, and then would turn around and teach the course on Wednesday nights. We were able to pay off all our $40,000 debt in one year. Because we didn't have any debt, Gina was able to leave her job at TD Auto Finance. Her job involved the collections side of the insurance world. She was the one that called you to collect the balance on loans people owed after their car was totaled. Contrary to popular belief, when a car is totaled, not all the balance will be paid off. She saw the dark side of money lending and the foolish decisions tens of thousands of people make in their finances. Someone will owe $30,000 on a $10,000 car because of rollover loans. So, she was the last person you wanted calling you. When she called you, that meant you owed a lot of money to the bank.

People would say the meanest things to her, blaming her, so she was glad to leave. She came and worked with me at my business, because work for me was on the no list. She would assist me and help me set limits on myself. Besides, who would not love to have their wife with them at work? In the years we had been married, I could count on one hand the times we were apart from each other.

Through our faith in God, he removed crutch after crutch and had me stand on my own. He carried me through separation and divorce and kept Stacey and I as friends. He kept us, as parents, focused on the betterment of our children, and we were blessed with smart, beautiful girls. He had delivered me from an identity crisis in the Navy when I believed I was nothing without them. He had given me a smoke-free life and delivered us from the quagmire of self-inflicted debt to financial peace. We realized Gina had been working her job just to pay off debt. After Gina quit her job, we knew, if we budgeted every cent, we could both enjoy a semi-retirement. Life was before us, and we could live a comfortable, blessed existence. That was the exact moment we would decide to sell it all and become missionaries for the Lord in the location of His choosing.

Lord, thank you for the mercy and miracles that are in my life every day. Help me to put aside the busyness of life and see you for who you are, the great deliverer and healer. The author and finisher of my faith.

Chapter 6

SPIRITUAL PATHS AND FAMILY TREES

Obedience comes with a steep price tag,
But the warranty is out of this world.

—Unknown

TO SAY MY MOTHER likes family history would be an understatement. Growing up, my family was always very close. We would have uncles, aunts, and cousins visit our home in South Carolina from time to time. A vacation to us was to go for a drive and stay with family in Georgia, South Carolina, North Carolina, Virginia, or maybe, if we were lucky, Uncle David down in Florida. If we ever asked my dad to go somewhere outside our five-state area he would respond with, "Leave the South? Why?"

Anything north of the Mason Dixon or west of the Mississippi River was no man's land, and there was no reason to cross it. My dad and his love for the South would always stay with me.

There's a saying we have in the South, "Southern born and Southern Bred, and when I Die, I'll be Southern Dead." There has always been something about sweet tea, fried chicken, biscuits, and collards that made me miss home. The weather always seemed to be nice, and fishing was always the best on that black water. The quiet and tranquil mountain trails of western North Carolina or the swamps of South Carolina and the Santee River catfish always bring good memories. Church on Sunday, and cookouts after the service, neighbors caring about neighbors, that was home.

Visiting Uncle David, who lived in Florida would be the only reason we would go there. Disney was there, but we never went. The first time I went to Disney was when I was twenty-one years old and married with no kids. I am not sure why we never went, but I knew it was costly back then, and on a pastor's salary at a small southern church, it was not possible. Our theme park of choice was Carowinds on the NC/SC border. My mother's parents were just a short drive from Charlotte to the park, and we loved it there.

Over the years, I would learn the world's definition of a family vacation would become more and more elaborate. It is so stressful today because we feel the need to pack so much into our time of rest that you almost need a vacation after your vacation. The years I lived in Florida with my kids, we went to Disney or SeaWorld, maybe twice a year. I better understand what quality family time is now. It is not about the destination, it's about the time that's spent with family. I remember who my aunts, uncles and cousins are because of the time I spent with them and from the family vacations we took to visit them. Memories of family are important, and we should always remember our past and where we came from. It's what defines who we are.

I needed to spend less time on the business side of life and more time on the relationship side. All too often, we head off in several different paths and we miss what God is trying to teach us. Life is a journey we all walk.

This is the best way I can describe our journey: God builds a path for each person's life. He first levels the ground we walk on with His grace and mercy to keep us steady. He gives us discernment to recognize and remove the potential stumbling points in our lives. Through the Holy Spirit, He sets guard rails up to keep us on the narrow path, by giving us Biblical wisdom and understanding of His word. He sets down firm paving stones on the path that fit together like a puzzle. The most important part of the process is you can only walk the path of life as fast as God builds it. If you try to move too fast with your plan, you get off the path, stumble, and lose your footing, or you make a wrong turn and crash through a guardrail.

As Gina and I began to understand His path for us to follow, we were careful not to move faster than He would lead us, and that was the hardest part. God was laying down stones for us to walk on, and these stones were vital in the formation of our spiritual walk. These stones were events and people that were put in our lives, helping keep us steady as we walked. Events like certain sermons we heard, or Scripture we read, and people God placed in our lives make up these stones in our path.

One such paving stone was when Gina and I had reached a point where we knew that serving God on a global scale was going to happen. When Gina and I were still dating, we had attended a class at Celebration Church that was on the Great Commission from the Gospel of Matthew. Throughout our study of these Scriptures, we saw the different levels of the Great Commission. The primary focus was on two kinds of people. There are those who are sent, and there are senders, but you had to be one of them. So, when we came to the mission's fork in our life path, we applied what we had learned from our pasts to help us make this decision. That seemingly small class we attended over a year ago became a solid truth that we could move forward on. We chose to be sent.

MATTHEW 28:16-20

16 Then the eleven disciples went away into Galilee, into a mountain where Jesus had appointed them.

17 And when they saw him, they worshipped him: but some doubted.

18 And Jesus came and spake unto them, saying, All power is given unto me in heaven and in earth.

19 Go ye therefore, and teach all nations, baptizing them in the name of the Father, and of the Son, and of the Holy Ghost:

20 Teaching them to observe all things whatsoever I have commanded you: and, lo, I am with you always, even unto the end of the world. Amen.

Now Jesus, who has been given *all power* instructs (Who?) His chosen followers to go out and (Do what?) teach new followers. (What do we teach them?) Everything He has taught us. Looking at everything He has just taught them from the beginning of His ministry to now, that is a lot. Now logic would dictate that this does not mean everyone in the world needs to start running around and head to the four corners of the globe at once, trampling all over each other. Sharing the good news of Jesus starts at home with your neighbors and your coworkers. In all four Gospels, there is a logic to Jesus and His ministry, there is a method to it all. In order to better understand the ending, you need to do your research and go back to the beginnings.

MATTHEW 10: 5-7

⁵ These twelve Jesus sent forth, and commanded them, saying, Go not into the way of the Gentiles, and into any city of the Samaritans enter ye not:

⁶ But go rather to the lost sheep of the house of Israel.

⁷ And as ye go, preach, saying, The kingdom of heaven is at hand.

He wants us to start at home, to start with our neighbors and our fellow countrymen. In the field of missions, some will go out into the field, and some will stay home. Each one of these roles is vital in spreading the Word. Some will spread funds where they are needed, and some will raise the funds for others to spread. In the world, this could be a potential stumbling block in some being jealous having to sit at home or pride for being on the front line of missions and doing it on your own power. Jesus also teaches about seed planting and the harvest from both sides.

JOHN 4:35-38

³⁵ Say not ye, There are yet four months, and then cometh harvest? behold, I say unto you, Lift up your eyes, and look on the fields; for they are white already to harvest.

³⁶ And he that reapeth receiveth wages, and gathereth fruit unto life eternal: that both he that soweth and he that reapeth may rejoice together.

37 And herein is that saying true, One soweth, and another reapeth.

38 I sent you to reap that whereon ye bestowed no labour: other men laboured, and ye are entered into their labours.

Jesus was telling them that the time is now. There is no time to waste. The harvesters are His disciples and the fields are the people of the world. He also points out that everyone receives wages because of the work, no matter what part they play. Some men will sow the seeds, some will water and care for the seed, some will remove the weeds from the heart of the seed, and some will reap the fruit.

Why does He tell them in verse 38 about reaping where another has sown, where someone else has done the work? One reason I believe is that He tells us to be aware that despite all the reaping you will do, someone else could have planted that seed. Someone else may have even died for that seed. The other is to tell us it is not about keeping track of your seeds or keeping a reaping-the-fruit score card.

Secondly, you will plant seeds and you may never see the fruit, but someone else will, and that needs to be okay also. Do not be discouraged if you are not directly involved in reaping because nothing you do for the Lord is in vain. In addition, do not take pride in reaping, as if you were the reason they have come. This can lead you down a dangerous and pride filled path of self-gratification, and that's not Biblical at all.

In 2016, Gina and I took a missions trip to Maine to assist in conducting a teen camp called, "True Love Waits." Most of the team had been visiting this area of Maine for years and had built relationships with the teens already. During that trip two girls came forward and told Gina that they wanted to give their hearts to the Lord. Now Gina had no idea why they came to her, but all we know is the Holy Spirit was moving that day. No one asked why, but instead, we all rejoiced together because it takes teamwork, the body, and the global church.

Jesus wants us to stop putting off the harvest and saying there is time. Be aware that we are not the only ones that hear the call to the harvest because Satan hears it also. Satan's harvest moves like a combine, and he is behind the wheel. The teeth of the combine are ISIS, Al-Shabaab, Al-Qaida, Hamas, Hizballah, and the PLO to name a few. The fuel for Satan's combine is hate, fear, confusion, and racism, to which we ourselves fuel it. The combine has been in action on many fronts from Kenya, Nigeria, and Israel, to Lebanon, Syria, and the USA with equal ferocity. Instead of bickering over coffee cup colors, Chick-fil-a, and who says Merry Christmas, we all need to get back to the task at hand and stop falling for these stupid distractions of the devil. We need to get back to the work of reconciling men to God through His Son, Jesus. It is what the harvest is all about, not our political point of view or the "Jesus chip" we carry on our shoulders. This is not a time for hate, fear, or confusion, because these things are not from God. Welcome to the front lines of the battle, the world is ready. It's time for us to get into the game.

Through all the life experiences that both Gina and I had: my leadership, teaching abilities, and travel experience through the US Navy, partnered with Gina's degrees in Business Management, Graphic Design, and her travel, God had put together a pretty good team with a wide range of abilities. Through prayer and discernment, we were chosen to be the deliverers and put ourselves out there, we just did not know where.

While we waited for God's answer of where, we would do business as usual and be aware of what God was showing us. It is amazing what you see when your focus is on the right things. We did have questions. How long should we wait? Answer: as long as it takes. There is no time limit on waiting, or age or ability when it comes to service to God. Moses was eighty years old when God chose him to deliver His people. I was currently only forty. God chooses the time and the place, and we must be alert and sensitive to His commands. As the song by John Waller says, "I will serve you while I'm waiting," and serve Him we did.

At East Pointe Church, we both signed up to participate in the church's discipleship program called Directions. The book contained eighteen weekly lessons; each lesson had five days in it. We would each be given a discipleship partner whom we would meet with on a set day of the week and cover our lesson in our book.

My Directions leader would be Ron Hall, a deacon at our church. I came to know him as a friend, mentor, and coach. Ron was instrumental in guiding me through the course and putting on the final touches in my direction towards missions. He was one of those paver stones God puts in our life walk; he was just the right person, at the right place, at the right time.

Think back to all the people you know that enriched your life at just the right time. People God used to guide you and set you on your firm foundation. When you slow down and think about all of them, the blessings become very clear. There are so many blessings you may have missed.

Gina was assigned to Shirley Walker, a friend from church. Shirley is so in tune with God and His greatness, everyone around her sees it on her face and in her daily walk with Him. She is a bright light whenever she walks into a room, a city on a hill. The Directions course may have looked easy, but it was far from that. It took daily commitment and dedication. Sure, you could fill in the blanks, read over the material, and go through the motions, but you'd only hurt yourself. Read the material, think about how it pertains to your daily life, and then apply it to your walk. Just like a gym workout, you get out of it what you put into it. You need to feel the burn of a good workout to see growth.

When you read your Bible, you can read it like a novel, but what do you get out of it? You can just open a daily passage and decide to apply it to your life, but how deep is your understanding of that one verse? Ask the Holy Spirit for wisdom and understanding, then open yourself up to Him. Men will study the Word of God their entire lives and never completely understand all of it. They will buy numerous study books and never be able to fully grasp what God is telling them. Some questions we will just have to ask God face to face when we see Him, and I am okay with that. Think about how many times you read a particular verse over the years, and how you always learn something different each time you read it. To me, that's wisdom and the ability to let God speak to me. That's the best part about it, you are always consuming the Word. Not reading it so you can have knowledge but reading it so you can be a better disciple of Him.

MATTHEW 5:6

"Blessed are those that hunger and thirst for Rightness for they shall be filled".

So many people walk around hungry for truth. They want to hold onto something that is real. They grab the emptiness and illusions from the world. It may satisfy them for a short while, but they will still be looking to fill the hole. Jesus fills the hole and builds onto it, and they grow stronger with a spiritual food that only Jesus can provide. Like doing the Directions course, the first thing needed is commit yourself to study the word, commit yourself to let God speak to you. If you're looking for an emotional high, go ride a roller coaster or watch a movie. If you want a relationship built on truth, listen to God.

Ron Hall and Shirley Walker were placed into our lives to provide stability at just the right time to help pave the path that would lead us where God wanted us. I began to think back on all the people that guided us in our walk and provided direction. Take some time to trace back all those people that guided you to a better understand were we came from, and how we got here. This is what I like to call my Spiritual Family Tree.

My mother was always quick to trace back our family tree to our European roots with modern technology. She would scan photos of great nieces, nephews, and great-great grandfathers to preserve them. Many of us kids today would ask why my mother would spend most of her time sorting through old pictures, spending endless hours writing down stories about our family. She wanted a reference for our family, so we wouldn't forget. My mother taught me that we need to be able to look back on our past and trace where we came from. We learn from our past and apply it to our future, just like a hereditary family tree. The spiritual history of our lives can be traced back like a spiritual family to be able to step back and look at all the spiritual connections that were made. If you follow them back, you will be surprised to see the blessings that will be revealed. One day, I started to trace back my spiritual family tree to the beginning and was surprised.

When it comes to Gina and my spiritual family tree, it would start with Darla who brought Gina and I together. The path that takes place after this is filled with blessings. Later in the book, you will learn more about these specific stories which create our family tree.

Our lives in Jacksonville were good and relatively easy. We were in the Word, studying, and praying for our children in their daily walk. We had paid off our debt, Gina had resigned from her job, and we sat down to prayerfully contemplate what our next move would be. Gina and I prayed with boldness, "God we are here for You. You have paved the way for us to be here, and we offer ourselves completely up to You for Your service."

There is something invigorating about the freedom of giving yourself completely over and being utterly exposed to God's will. No excuses, no stories, just letting God do what He wants with us and strip everything we would use as a crutch and remove it from our lives. We prayed, "God, take everything and make it Yours so it would not hinder us. I want You to make us uncomfortable, I want You to move our feet. Break our hearts for what breaks Yours." I was so tired of living in fear of men that I wanted to face it head on.

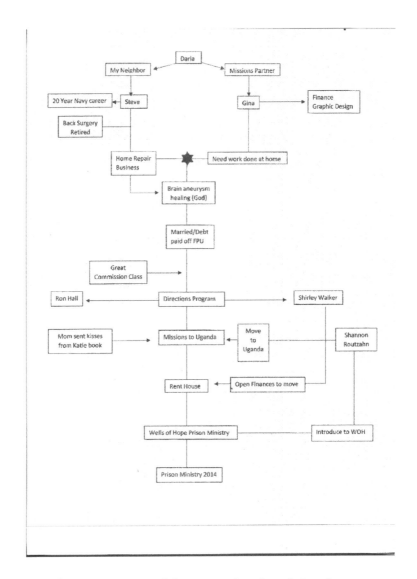

We knew we would serve the Lord in the place of His choosing, and over the next few months, we narrowed it down to two places. One was Cameroon in the northwest corner of Africa and Uganda in the central belt, located on the equator, bordering Lake Victoria, and Kenya. I had heard of some groups in Cameroon that were well spoken of, and Gina had been to Uganda and Zimbabwe before. From my travels in the Navy, I had spent most of my time in the French-speaking, western side of Africa. Countries like Nigeria, Democratic Republic of Congo (DRC), and Sierra Leone, most of the time fighting people who were trafficking drugs and humans, both which were very lucrative for modern-day terrorist organizations.

Most of the areas we were in were okay, but nothing had jumped out at us. We requested God's intervention in our decision.

PROVERBS 16:3

Commit thy works unto the Lord, and thy thoughts shall be established.

Our missionary friend, Shannon Routzahn from Celebration Church, who we supported financially, was home on a break from her work in Zimbabwe. We had invited her over to our house for dinner, and she shared stories of the work she was doing and how things were going. She then thanked us for supporting her and informed us that she would be making a ministry change from Zimbabwe to work with a group called Kids at Heart in Uganda, asking if we would still be willing to support her. We were excited for her and shared with her our prayers to serve as missionaries, our choices we had to make, and that she may have been part of that choice. Was God telling us something? A few days later, we received a package in the mail from my mother. Now before my mother knew of our mission's plans, she had mailed Gina and me a book, and when we opened it, we knew where we would go. The title of the book was "*Kisses from Katie,*" it is about a young girl that helps children in, you guessed it... Jinja, Uganda. The day we received the book, we knew God was telling us something. Now, knowing where our new home would be, we began to make a list to prepare ourselves for the transition.

Our first task was to deal with all the extra stuff we had. Twenty-plus years of moving all over the world, I had collected some things. We had sold some stuff to pay off our debt while we were working through Dave Ramsey's Financial Peace University. With a new focus and drive, we started to sell off our stuff at a record pace. I never realized how much time it took to manage a house full of things. Cleaning, organizing, preserving takes a lot of time. We had around seven garage sales, in which we sold the trailer and mostly all the tools. We were now able to park both cars in the garage and had room to spare. It was invigorating to lighten the load and not be tied down. We would learn to streamline our life and spend our time with the girls more wisely.

When we started to tell people about our plans, we started with those that were closest to us. We shared it with our girls, Ashton, and Gabby, because we wanted to get their thoughts on it. We showed them on a map where Uganda was and described it the best we could. We sat down and laid out our thoughts on our choices and how we came to this decision. They seemed very excited about it and started asking questions that we didn't have the answers to. "How much does it cost to live there? What kind of house will you have? Is there power? Do you have a bathroom?"

Ummmm... We weren't sure yet, but they were good questions. Using my military organizational skills, we started to make a list based off those questions that would be our minimum wants list. Would we want power? Yes. Communication via computer was vital to our supporters and ministry needs. Did we need water? Yes, we could get bottled water or boil it, but that would require extra effort. Toilets? Most bathrooms were the outhouse style, and we could adjust if we had to; it was Africa.

We began to make lists of things that needed to be done. By far, the most popular topic of conversation was, "How long do you plan on being there? Who are you going to be working with?"

We would tell people that we were not exactly sure how long we would stay or whom we'd work with, but we would just let the Holy Spirit lead us. They would then give us the uneasy smile and just nod their heads, "Oooo-kaaay, sounds good," like we were crazy or something. We did not like to put limits on what God had planned for us. That tended to make people a little nervous, talking so openly about the Holy Spirit moving us and being willing to go anywhere.

As my Ugandan friends would tell me, "Americans don't do anything without a plan and weeks of notice," and that is true. This can be good and bad, but that wasn't how we were. We were fluid to move with the Holy Spirit, but we would still need to write down plans for our future. We knew we were going to Uganda, but we could end up in South Sudan, Kenya, or who knows where. We were always worried that if we set cemented plans with dates and places, supporters wouldn't be as flexible as we were or would take it the wrong way if God presented a new fork in the road. We did not want confusion or hurt feelings for anyone.

Our friend Jill Dykstra, whose freedom to follow the Holy Spirit is so fluid, and so flexible that the Holy Spirit changes her direction like some people change underwear, encouraged us not to worry too much about what men think, but instead be sensitive to the Holy Spirit. Go ahead and make plans in accordance with the Holy Spirit, write them down for man, just do it in pencil. Uganda was God's chosen starting point, and we began to prepare for it. With the help of East Pointe Church, through their direct support and various fundraisers, we were able to raise more than enough money for everything we needed.

With our new-found time, Gina and I were able to take a marriage enrichment course with our good friends and supporters, Keith and Connie Korte. It was the perfect class at the perfect time. Keith and Connie's class was a great example of being missionaries in the local field in Jacksonville. Not everyone will move to Africa or Asia, but they serve at the home front, preparing others to go. They use their talents and drive to serve and prepare others mentally, spiritually, and financially. We used their marriage class to strengthen our relationship while separated from our home base, and we have used it to build on each other. Sometimes I believe the marriage class is what got us through our first year in Uganda.

Some may ask, "Why would you leave your comfort zone and put that kind of strain on your relationship on purpose?"

Easy. Jesus commands it. Jesus also left His comfort zone on high to come to earth for me, so why would I not leave mine? To lay down one's life for another means to put the interests and wishes of others ahead of your own. It implies that to obey Christ and carry out His intentions is more desirable than doing my own thing.

We spent some time laying everything out in our minds to make sure we were not missing something. Gina and I had been brought together by a medical miracle. My days of physical labor were sadly over. I now had found out I had a two-plus year wait on the VA to hear my case on disability compensation for my back. God, through Dave Ramsey, had helped us pay off all our debt in record time. He provided us with training and preparation through well placed mentors and gave us well placed signs of the direction in which we should go. After all the miracles God did in our lives, it was easy to make the choice… or was it?

The decision to leave the girls behind for our first year would be the hardest decision I would have to make. I was sorry I missed a lot of events in their lives while in the Navy, and I always felt a loss over it, sad that I could not go back and change the past. On the other hand, I had also realized that I always provided for them while I was gone for my work. My career gave us a future, a roof, food, clothes, schooling, and a life. I was and still am a provider and I did the best I could with what I had. Was I sorry? Yes. Would I do some things differently? Yes. Did I have regrets? No.

Firstly, I realized I had been carrying that guilt around for so many years, and so I asked the girls to forgive me for that, and they have. Ashton and Gabby are the most beautiful girls in the world, precious to their father on Earth and their Father in Heaven. As time went on, I learned that provision for your family is important, but I must have a level set on what's provision and what is excess. Secondly, I learned that it's not just the destination, but time spent that is most important. That time will not stop when they turn eighteen years old. They do not stop being my children. Because of the Gospel of Jesus Christ, we will have our whole lives on earth and in heaven together forever. Thirdly, we needed to make the remaining time on earth count for something. Being a provider is not just taking care of worldly needs, but, more importantly, being a spiritual provider. To show them how to live a life worth living for God and not for men, and that takes faith and getting out of our comfort zone. I could not ask them to go all in for a God that I was not willing to go all in for myself. I wanted to be that example and live a life worth living for God and them. So, in the future when I am gone, that will be the legacy I will leave for them. A godly example of a godly man. Father, Husband, and Son. To God be the glory.

Our plans of service to the Lord would also involve the girls greatly. Their future was wide open, and their road would be paved in prayer. I will be their father forever, and through them, I would better define myself as being a man of faith. They were teaching me a lesson without knowing it. We pray for their path and their walk with God daily. It all made me ask myself, how far was I willing to go? How much would we be able to forsake? All? Nothing? Part?

Faith will lead us into some dark places in our life, but God promises we will not go through it alone. He will be the lamp unto our feet and a light unto our path, and as we would soon find out, we would always need a light on the Dark Continent.

Throughout my career in the Navy, I had been in many stressful situations and was under a lot of pressure to excel. We began to question ourselves, why us? Did we have what it takes? Living alone in a third world country was very different than anything we had ever known. What would people think of us? Would they support us? All good questions that needed answers. There was no support group, no tour guide, no protection. As we say in the Navy, we were the tip of the spear, on the front lines, and it would be God and us. I could think of no better place to be.

2 TIMOTHY 2:1-4

1Thou therefore, my son, be strong in the grace that is in Christ Jesus.

²*And the things that thou hast heard of me among many witnesses, the same commit thou to faithful men, who shall be able to teach others also.*

³*Thou therefore endure hardness, as a good soldier of Jesus Christ.*

⁴*No man that warreth entangleth himself with the affairs of this life; that he may please him who hath chosen him to be a soldier.*

Lord, help us to focus on You, Your Word, and not the world. Strengthen us on the inside, give us the direction to follow and the compassion to serve. Lord, may Your ministry give others light and those that hear our testimony give you glory. Thank You for making us soldiers on the front lines."

Chapter 7

FIGHT OR FLIGHT: "WELCOME TO MY SPIRITUAL DOJO."

(Photo taken from the Author)
"Don't ask God for an easier life; ask Him to make you a stronger person."

-Francis Chan

Have you ever had a moment in your life when you felt completely exposed? A time so terrifying, or so awkward, you wanted to just melt away? In the Navy, I learned that these moments can be described as "fight or flight." A moment where a personal decision must be made: do I stay and fight or do I run away? (flight) Every time one of these decisions needs to be made, you are forced to look inside yourself and choose which one to do. When you choose fight, to trust in God, you build onto your faith and choose not to live in fear of this opportunity God has provided. In flight, you will retreat, re-evaluate, and make an adjustment for the future. When we moved to Uganda, Gina and I were spiritually exposed to the elements around us, and we were open to whatever God had in store for us.

PROVERBS 3:5-6

5. Trust in the Lord with all thine heart; and lean not on your own understanding.

6. In all thy ways acknowledge him, and he shall direct thy paths.

On our first visit to Uganda in Sep 2013, we were there for four weeks of work and a week of rest and reflection before we headed back. We went there to stretch our wings, to push ourselves to the limit, and to let God take us wherever He wanted. When we arrived in Entebbe Airport, we were greeted by Shannon Routzahn, our friend and fellow missionary from Jacksonville, Florida, and Wells of Hope Director, Francis Ssuubi. From the day we landed, it was go-time. We were there for a five-week fact-finding mission to see what God wanted us to do. Shannon had introduced us to Wells of Hope (WOH) in Uganda, and we wanted to give them a test drive. WOH Ministry is in fact the first of its kind on the continent of Africa. They had established first a prison ministry that visited several prisons in and around the Kampala area. They'd also built Wells of Hope Academy, a boarding school for children of those prisoners.

On our first visit to Murchison Bay prison in Kampala, Uganda, we were completely out of our element. Here we were, about to enter a prison in a third world country, to minister to some of the inmates. Before we came to Uganda, Gina and I had been watching a show called *Locked up Abroad* on Netflix. It is a show with stories about people who were locked up in some of the world's worst prisons and in the direst situations, and Uganda was one of them.

As we waited outside to enter, we studied everything the people we were with were doing; we wanted to know all the correct procedures to perform. We took comfort in the fact that, being white, we would stand out and not be mistaken as inmates, but there was still some worry. Were these guys hardened criminals? Killers even? The Murchison Bay Prison church was an open building with about seventy-five men sitting on mats and wooden benches. After we sang a few worship songs in Luganda, the local language, the Wells of Hope Director Francis Ssuubi introduced us and invited me up to speak and share a message with the men.

What??? Are you kidding? What am I supposed to say? How long do I have? Who are these men? Is there anything I shouldn't say? Sheer terror had taken over. I was just some random guy from Florida; I was no public speaker, nor a pastor!

Francis looked me in the eye and gave me the answer which we now have come to live by: "Just let the Holy Spirit lead you."

Well, as I walked the ten feet to the podium, the Holy Spirit led me right to a Scripture my friend and pastor, Mark McGaughey made me memorize over a year before in our men's group at East Pointe Church.

As I stood in front of the men and opened my Bible, I turned to 1 Thessalonians 5.

1 THESSALONIANS 5:14-25 (KJV)

[14] *Now we exhort you brethren, warn those that are unruly, comfort the feebleminded, support the weak, be patient with all men.*

[15] *See that no one renders evil for evil upon any man, but ever follows that which is good both unto yourselves and to all men.*

[16] *Rejoice evermore.*

[17] *Pray without ceasing,*

¹⁸*In all things give thanks; for this is the will of God in Christ Jesus concerning you.*

¹⁹*Quench not the Spirit.*

²⁰*Despise not prophecies.*

²¹*Prove all things; hold fast that which is good.*

²²*Abstain from any appearance of evil.*

²³*And the very God of peace sanctify you wholly; and I pray your whole spirit, soul, and body be preserved blameless until the coming of our Lord Jesus Christ.*

²⁴*Faithful is He who calls you, who also will do it.*

²⁵*Brethren, pray for us.*

I went straight to it, talking about what men of God do, how we can lift up and encourage each other. I taught them how we can fellowship with each other and be leaders through our faith, as well as how we should test everything, prove all things against the Word of God, and hold on to what is God's truth. Gina and I had survived our first brush-in with prison, and it seemed to be well received. When we first thought about being missionaries, we prayed for God to never let us get comfortable, to never settle down. We wanted Him to take us out of our comfort zone and put us in His zone. Be careful what you pray for because you will get it.

I had taken an opportunity God had provided and applied something that I learned from my past. This would become a practice I would use daily. During our men's group at East Pointe Church in Jacksonville, Mark McGaughey had us memorizing scripture. MP4 was more than a Bible study on Saturdays, it was a men-of-God support group. During the meetings with these men, they would lay the spiritual groundwork of who I would be that day in prison. We would eat doughnuts, drink coffee, pray for each other, and study the Word of God. It was a time to strip yourself of the world's definition of a man and build yourself as a man of God.

The world has many views of what a man should be. A man is strong, silent, and never asks for help because he always has the answers. He is always handsomely dressed and business-like, but not afraid to get his hands dirty. He is honest and straightforward but has an allure of mystery at the same time. He is rugged, loves the outdoors, and is a world traveler, but also likes to stay home with the family. He is as stern as a judge but gentle as a puppy. He is a romantic and a poet at heart, but at the same time is strong, silent, and confident. I personally do not know one man who fits this description at all. Not ever and in no way does this resemble real life.

As men, we gauge ourselves off what the world expects of us, and believe me, we will never achieve it. We will never reach it because we are thinking too small. I realize now I will never again set my expectations of a man at such a low level again. I must pray for God's wisdom and strength. I must pray for His guidance and patience. When things go well, I will thank Him for the blessings. When things do not go my way, I will thank God for my lesson and direction. As a society, we search for the perfect role model from TV shows and movies, and they are not there. God sent us the perfect role model, His Son, Jesus Christ.

The Wells of Hope Ministry had many different levels and working parts. The Director Mr. Francis Ssuubi was at one time a prisoner at Murchison Bay Prison in Kampala. A business partner had a disagreement with him and paid a policeman 5,000 Ugandan Shillings ($2.50 USD) to have him arrested and wrongfully accused. He spent sixty-three days in prison, and God delivered to him the groundwork that would become Wells of Hope Ministries. What began as a negative for Mr. Ssuubi became a God-ordained mission.

(Photo taken from the Author)
(Left to Right) Marjorie, Ellen Ssuubi, Francis
Ssuubi, Emmanuel Ceaser, Pauline, Peter, Steve
Gant
Gina Gant, Sarah, Emmanuel's wife, Doris, Lucy,
(2014)

WOH is broken down into three basic levels. Over our time there we were able to be very productive in all levels of the ministry. As we participated at each one of the levels, we learned more about ourselves, our limits and more importantly, our God.

PHASE 1: PRISON MINISTRY

Remember those in prison, as you were their fellow prisoners and those who were mistreated, as if you yourselves were suffering. (Hebrews 13:3)

Gina and I conducted a Bi-weekly prison discipleship program at four prisons in Luzira: Death Row, Boma General Prison, Murchison Bay Men's and Luzira Women's.

We had a time to worship with local songs, music, and study of the Word of God. Our current study took us through the four Gospels, Matthew, Mark, Luke, and John. We studied the life of Jesus from the birth of John the Baptist to the Great Commission, verse by verse. We believed that not only were the men getting a deeper knowledge of the Word, but the verse-by-verse study opened eyes to a whole new level of understanding of Jesus, the disciples, and the Pharisees. It led to an understanding of how things fell into place, how truly everything happened for a reason, and how God's perfect plan unfolded.

During our visits, we got to know the inmates well and shared in many of their testimonies and struggles. When an inmate is in prison and has not heard from his or her family in some time, they request what we call a welfare visit. When I say, "not heard from his or her family," this means that they haven't seen their families in years, sometimes not at all. Some of these inmates never get a visitor, ever. The cost for someone to travel to visit can be a month's wages, and when they do visit, they culturally feel they must bring something for the inmate, which can be costly. When an inmate gets a visitor, it is a big deal.

One of these times was shared with us during a testimony at our Sunday church service at Condemned (Death Row) Prison. An inmate said in his testimony that the last time he saw his daughter was when he was arrested, she was two years old. He testified that she came to visit him a few days ago, and he was so excited to see her. She was now seventeen years old and in secondary school (High School). He was so happy to see her and her sisters that also came. I personally would have been a wreck after fifteen years of no family contact, but it was such a blessing in his life, and he gave God all the glory for everything that had happened.

When it came to a welfare visit, there were a few guidelines to doing a child search for a prisoner. The inmate must have been convicted of a crime, serving at least five years in prison, and still have at least five years left on their sentence. We delivered the request forms to the welfare officer at the prison for distribution to those who need it. The welfare officer knew which inmates were present and eligible for the program. Once the inmate filled out the form, he was to list each child by mother, age if known, spelling of the name, caretaker contact numbers, and draw out a general map to locate the area. There were a few things you could notice about the guidelines and form. Each prisoner must have been convicted of a crime, not just waiting on a court date. Large populations of the prison were awaiting trial. Some men we knew had been in prison for three or four years and had not been to court yet. Imagine being in prison for four years and have never even been convicted. No one knew why the system took so long, but it did. There were lawyers from outside that came in and did pro-bono cases daily. They did what they could to help move the process along and clear out some of the cells. We met one young lady at the front gate from the UK on one of our visits, who said she was currently handling over 1,000 cases herself, for free. It seemed like such an overwhelming task to work on one person at a time, but it was the calling some had, just like delivering the Gospel. It may not have seemed like a lot, but the ripple effect it made on the world was enormous.

During the form process we learned that some men still had multiple wives and multiple children from each of them. This practice was not uncommon, but slowly going away with the introduction of a better, Christian worldview.

The inmates would write down their best guess of the names and ages of the children from memory. It seemed like an easy task, but since most of the children's birthdays were not formally recorded, they really didn't know. We also realized that once you were in prison, time seemed to stand still. Years can go by without notice or change in routine. Years flew by like months. One inmate told us, "I know it's Friday because you and Gina are here, because you're always here on Friday". This touched us so much because one of our goals for the prison ministry was to be regulars, so they would know we are coming, and they could look forward to it. This is not a knock against them, but a lot of prison ministries came at odd times or scheduled a time and were late or didn't show up at all. We wanted to show them we didn't come when it was comfortable for us, but we set a time to revolve around the inmates, because they were important to God and us.

Once we had the forms completed with all information, we collected them by region of the country. When we got enough children from one area, we could start to plan a trip to that area and look for their children.

PHASE 2: TRACING CHILDREN

In the same way, it is not my heavenly fathers will that even one of these little ones should perish. (Matthew 18:14)

Tracing children is the process of taking clues from the inmate and driving to remote locations to find the missing children of the inmate. When we planned a tracing trip to an area, we collected the forms and maps and got volunteers to go out with us. Some trips would be great distances, so we had to plan how long it would take to contact each family and find where they were located. A road may only seem like 120 miles away, but due to poor road conditions, a three-hour trip could take up to six or eight hours. If the area was some distance away, we would plan several days to complete the job. Once we located the child and family members, we interviewed them and took pictures of the children and family. The most vulnerable children would be considered first for sponsorship. If they met the criteria, we could get a sponsor to send money to send them to Kampala to live at Wells of Hope Academy. During our interview, we assessed their health condition, schooling situation, and whether they were eating. We couldn't take every child, and part of our job was to decide which ones we could help, and it was not a fun job at all. This usually meant the girls may get looked at first because of sexual abuse and the chances of being married off early. Children in some areas were also vulnerable to be hired out for labor or sold as a child sacrifice to witch doctors.

Just because a child was not attending school, that did not mean they would be taken into the program. We were not there to break up families but to encourage them to stay together. In some cases, the child could be the only provider for the elderly caretaker and the younger siblings that all lived under the same roof. I know it does not seem fair to have a ten-year-old girl cook and clean for her grandparents and younger siblings, but that is just the way life is in many countries, and that is normal. For this reason, each case had to be handled individually. Once a child was chosen for the academy, and we were able to secure a sponsor, the family had to bring the child to the academy to show their commitment to the program and to demonstrate that we didn't just take them from their homes.

Some families we visited did not know that their incarcerated family member was even alive or in prison, so some were quite shocked to hear they were still around. We got some strange looks sometimes—two white people walking up to a village and saying, "We're from Wells of Hope. Your son who's in prison has sent us to check on you." Many times, it ended in tears of joy to hear that their son, brother, or father was alive. We explained who we were, and we informed the family that we needed to find the children a sponsor before they were accepted into the Wells of Hope Academy in Kampala. Upon our return, we went to the prison and sat down with each inmate, giving them the pictures of their children, and telling them messages from their family and friends. They were now able to keep the pictures of their families in their cells to remember them. We also started taking pictures of their parents, family, and friends they might remember from their past to have a photo of them as well. We hoped this helped bridge the gap between families and the inmates in prison. Once they were released, we prayed they have confidence that they could return home and reunite with their families.

PHASE 3: WELLS OF HOPE ACADEMY

The academy was set up for children of prisoners and provided them with everything they needed. A $35.00 monthly donation supplied a child with a dormitory assignment, a bed, uniforms, education, food, counseling, and Bible studies. Three times a year, all the children were taken by bus to the prisons to visit their parents. A normal prison visit would last about thirty minutes in a darkened room, and they would yell through a screen, surrounded by everyone else yelling over each other. Wells of Hope Ministries had such a good working relationship with the prison and staff, that they were able to improve the children's rights to visit their parents.

During a Wells of Hope visit, the children got to sit on mats, face to face with the parents, and share food together, pray for each other, and share stories. Some of the WOH teachers were also there as chaperones and got to talk to the parents in makeshift parent-teacher meetings. The children shared family stories, grade reports, and school happenings, while parents got caught up on giving advice, parental wisdom, and just loving on them. They were able to visit for about three hours in place of the standard thirty minutes. At the end of each term during their holiday, the children could go home to visit their family in the village to maintain good family relationships. The children even gave the village family reports on how their father and mother were doing in prison and share stories.

PHASE 4: GRANDMOTHER/ GRANDFATHER VISITS

Since Gina and I had started with WOH, we have been able to try a pilot program of assisting grandparents, who most of the time were the children's caregivers, in visiting their son or daughter in prison. The main means of transportation was either by a taxi (van) or Boda Boda (small motorcycle taxi). Our ministry was to drive to the hard-to-reach areas of Uganda and provide a safe means of transportation for the elderly. We got to see the grandparents, pick them up, and take them to the prison for an extended visit. The same rules applied for the grandparents as the children; they also got to sit down and speak face to face to their child for sometimes two to three hours instead of the standard thirty minutes.

During their grandparent visit, Gina and I would go to visit with the prisoners that were sick in the infirmary and pray with them. During one grandmother visit, we spent some great time reading and praying for patients at the prison hospital. In all God had us doing, we were way out of our comfort zones and loving it. We went from bed to bed to talk and pray for each prisoner. As I approached one bedridden patient, I lay my hand on him, and he had a look of surprise on his face. I asked him what I could pray for him about.

He said, "My leg is infected."

I looked down at my hand, and it was directly on his open wound. The prisoner translator had a look of fear for me on his face, but I didn't flinch at all. I prayed for him, read some scripture, and he thanked me for coming all this way to see him.

We moved up to the roof where many men were sitting outside to get fresh air. Gina and I walked to the center of the group and started to talk and pray for them. The translator was still in the doorway, afraid to enter the area. He was afraid to enter because we were in the middle of the Tuberculosis (TB) ward isolation area. We told them it was ok, and we continued on with our prayers. Praise be to God, no sickness.

Gina and I never seemed to have any fear and loved the feeling of praying in boldness. I knew that God was moving in the hearts and lives of these men and women and although we may never see the results, we knew hearts and minds were being changed for God. We were watering seeds.

On the drive home, we tried to talk to the grandparent as much as possible because some never had anyone to talk to. Sometimes we were the only adult conversation they had with all the grandchildren around. It was a nice chance to share with them the love of Jesus and why we did what we did.

We got back late one night from dropping a grandmother off. It was about a seven-hour round trip but well worth it. It was getting dark as we prepared to drive the three hours back. We had made about ten turns into the distant bush areas with no idea how to get back to the city. The grandmother told us to take a different road back and would lead us back to the main road. She said, "It will be easier, just drive straight this way, and you will run right into the main road."

Oh, okay. Not sure why we did not take that road before? We learned why shortly after leaving the grandmother's house. Her definition of "easier" and mine were vastly different. It was an easier direction, but the worst road I had ever been on, or so I thought.

What stood out to me that night as we four-wheeled through the middle of nowhere was that we would occasionally drive by a person who was standing on the side of the road, covering their eyes with their hands. I first thought they were playing hide and seek like an ostrich, then I realized they were shielding their eyes form my head lights to keep their night vision as they walked.

Jesus, three friends, a whistle, and knife was all we had. Driving in the complete darkness in the African back country, check. Bucket list item completed!

Lord, thank you for life's timely lessons, even when we do not know we are learning. Thank you for extending our boundaries and stretching us to meet you where you are. Help us to be open, and to be flexible in getting out of our comfort zone to be used by you.

(Photo taken from the Author)

Me and my Building Construction Teacher Mr. Oates when I took 1st place in the regional competition.

(Photo taken by the Author)

Mom and Dad with Ashton and Gabrielle in Rockhill, SC.

(Photo taken from the Author)

Ashton And Gabrielle modeling picture.

(Photo taken from the Author)

A favorite spot for me when on deployment, Relaxing on the beach with a Beer and cigar in Panama, South America. (2008)

(Photo taken from the Author)

Working hard and playing hard. New Year's Eve Africa. (2009)

(Photo taken from the Author)

Talking foreign policy, favorite port visits, and Rugby with a foreign national. (2007)

(Photo taken from the Author)

Posing for a picture on board USS Samuel B. Roberts FFG 58. The best ship and crew in the fleet. (2010)

(Photo taken by the Author)

Visiting a prisoner's family in the village of Serere in the Eastern part of Uganda. The people were so happy to see us. You can see the women holding Gina's hand. The gentleman with the hat simply asked if I would be his friend. (2014)

(Photo taken by Gina Gant)

Spending time with the children at Wells of Hope Academy.

(Photo taken by the Author)

Talking scripture with some of the prisoners on Death Row. The men in condemned section were always so hopeful even though they faced the possibility of execution daily.

(Photo taken by some random person)

Relaxing by the Indian Ocean after our long drive to Mombasa Kenya.

(Photo taken by Gina Gant)

Visiting a family in the area of Karamoja in the Northeastern corner of Uganda. This was still one of the most underdeveloped areas in Eastern Africa. Clothing was still optional for many.

Chapter 8

BOOTS ON THE GROUND

Missions is not the ultimate goal of the church, worship is. Missions exist because worship doesn't. Worship is ultimate, not missions, because God is ultimate, not man.

—John Piper
"Let the Nations be Glad"

I LIKE TO CALL MYSELF a habitual line crosser. When I see a line, I must cross it. When I see a challenge, I want to overcome it. After returning home from our five-week vision trip to Uganda, we started our three months of preparations and fundraising. We were as prepared as God was going to have us. We were loved and prayed over by our friends, family, and church. We headed to the airport in Jacksonville, FL on December 31st, 2013. We would go from Jacksonville to Chicago to Istanbul, Turkey, to Kagali, Rwanda, then back up to Kampala, Uganda. We left Jacksonville wearing shorts in warm weather and landed in Chicago for layover #1, in snow and ten-degree weather. We landed at Entebbe airport in Central Uganda after a total of thirty-two hours, twenty-four of those hours in the air. Our first full year in Uganda began on January 1st, 2014, at 4:00 am. Our friends Ivan and Goodwin met us at the airport and drove us to Shannon's house to stay for a few days and sleep off the jet lag. What a blessing it was to have Shannon living in Uganda and provide us a stress-free place to start. It was like God placed her there to ease us into the transition. He was once again paving our way.

On our five-week fact-finding trip the year before, we had already secured a house to move into that met all the needs on our list of the three P's: power, plumbing, and protection. The day before we flew back from that five-week trip we were also able to purchase all the household things we needed all at one time from a family returning to Australia. As we went to their house to see the furniture, I was a little worried about the type and condition of furniture we would see. Gina is pretty picky when it comes to household goods, so I had my fingers crossed. Not buying things as a package deal would mean we would have to shop for every plate, fork, towel, and sheet. In a third world country, that could take months. To my delight, she loved everything and was very excited. The family that was selling was scheduled to move back to Australia six days after we landed in Kampala the next year to start our first year. When we landed, we picked up the furniture, and the Australian family boarded a plane. God's perfect timing.

Some of the hardest things about moving to a foreign country is having a trusted place to start, finding a suitable place to live. Also buying all your household items one by one can take all year and be very stressful. Less than two weeks into our first full year, we were already moved in and ready to go to work.

Gina and I enjoyed our first few days in our rented home in Kyanja. We dedicated our first two weeks to get all our personal things completed, like getting the house, moving all the furniture from one house to another, getting power and water on, shop for and buy transportation, and also learn to drive in town. The furniture was pretty much set up and we were getting settled in.

Shopping was one thing that I did not expect to be that hard, but it was. In my many years of travel in the Navy, I was a pro at haggling for the lowest price. As we shopped for a vehicle, we knew from our trip last year that we would need something that could get to some far-out areas and handle some extremely rough terrain.

When we had been tracing last year, we traversed some roads that more closely resembled dry riverbeds than roads. We purchased a 1998 Toyota Surf; it was the foreign version of the Toyota 4Runner. It had more ground clearance, four-wheel drive, room for six, and a luggage rack on the roof. As I mentioned, driving in Uganda was going to take a certain amount of adjustment on my part. I was learning to use the left side of the road and driving from the right side of the car, but driving in Kampala, the capital city would take nerves of steel and blindfolds for all passengers.

The driving in Uganda is so aggressive that it makes downtown New York City at rush hour look more like Pleasantville on a Sunday afternoon. If you do not stay bumper to bumper with the car in front of you, twenty cars will pass, grind, and/or bump into you. There are no lines on the streets, no lanes, no stop signs. Streetlights are a new concept and are catching on in the downtown areas, but most don't pay them any mind. The sidewalk is also considered a driving lane.

The pecking order of traffic is simple: the most aggressive drivers here are the people with UG on their license plate. UG stands for Uganda Government. We were warned about them. The largest trucks also have the right of way, no matter what because they are just bigger. Look out mostly for the big trucks from Kenya, which have been driving through the night to make a delivery. You can spot them fairly easy as they are chewing on roasted coffee beans with bloodshot eyes. No sleep, and sometimes no brakes.

Next in the order would be the taxi vans, which are the second largest menace on the road. They will drive around you, over you, and through you to get to where they need to go, which is usually to stop right in front of you to get their next passenger. Private cars are next, and the junkier the car, the more right of way it has. No one wants to tangle with a car that looks like it just fell off a cliff, because you can tell they do not care.

Last in the motorized food chain is a staple in the Uganda countryside and the number-one menace on the road, and that is the Boda Boda. There are two types of Bodas, a 50-cc motorcycle and a bicycle with a padded seat. The Boda Boda got its name from the early days of the bicycle version. They would transport passengers sitting on the back from one district border to another, so they called them border-to-borders or Boda Bodas. The bumper of your car could be almost touching the car in front of you, and they will find a way to zig zag around you. As soon as traffic stops, they swarm like roaches all around you, sometimes making moving difficult. They drive without a care in the world and cause more fatalities than any other means of transportation in this country, causing an estimated 200 injuries a day.

The bottom of the food chain is the pedestrian. If you are walking, you take your life in your own hands. There are no real sidewalks or really any crosswalks, so you are at risk. If you are hit, it is your fault for being in the way—even if you are on the sidewalk, you can be hit because it's part of the road.

Almost all vehicles in Uganda come used from Japan. I would say seventy-five percent of cars on the road are Toyotas. When it comes to cars, most things are the same except for two very different elements. The steering wheel is on the right, and they drive on the left. The first time I ever drove, we went out our gate, up the hill and turned right, away from town. We drove a few hours out into the countryside just to get a feel for driving on the left. Gina was always the navigator and gave directions so I could focus on driving the streets and navigating potholes and people. I would constantly have to tell myself "drive on the left, drive on the left." I turned the windshield wipers on more than once, thinking it was the turn signal. I had been driving since I was about fifteen years old and considered myself a pretty good driver, but nothing prepared me for driving in Uganda.

Growing up in South Carolina, driving on back roads, and mudding in my truck was second nature. As a teenager, I had learned a whole new way of driving, like reading ruts, analyzing the depth of mud and potholes. Just like in life, when you're in the deep mud, you need to keep moving, don't stop or you will sink. If your tires begin to spin, do not stomp on the gas or you will dig yourself in good, and when I mean good, that's bad.

One particular drive in Uganda, we were on our way to pick up a grandmother and take her for to see her son in prison. We were following the directions to her house and came to her road—when I say "road," it looked more like a goat path. We turned down the hill toward her house and because of all the rain we began to slide downhill. We did not slide very fast, but enough to know there was nothing we could do. With trees a foot away from us on both sides as we slid, all we could do was hold on. Steering was pretty much useless but was more like a slow rudder on a boat and moved very little. We could only see about twenty feet in front of us because of all the low hanging branches. The two options were that we would come to a clearing and run into a house and that would stop us, or I would try to steer into a tree and that would stop us also. Both situations involved stopping, but damage would result from both. I had no idea what was ahead of me; due to my lack of vision, I could not see anything. What if there was a drop off or a house ahead? Fear of that unknown made me think about bailing and aiming for a tree, but why? Was I so afraid of what could happen? I decided to trust and believe that we would be able to stop. Somehow, for about 100 yards, we did not hit anything and got to the bottom of the hill where we stopped safely.

In our lives we often lose sight of things ahead of us, or we are not sure what God's plan is. We tend to bail out early and count ourselves lucky, but that way, we could miss an opportunity to serve Him, or, even more importantly, see God come through in a big way. Trust in the Lord, lean on Him, and serve Him while you wait. Sometimes you just have to sit there and trust that God is steering you.

Driving back up the hill was also a challenge. However, we ended up spinning and sliding with confidence and ability, thanks to God and my experiences from South Carolina. When we brought the grandmother home the next time, we decided to park at the top of the hill and walk her down the muddy hill to her house to make sure she was ok. God had delivered us from a serious situation before, but there was no reason to push Him. As we walked down the hill, we were slipping and sliding the whole way down. The grandmother walked in front of us like she was walking on pavement. She kept turning to check and make sure we were ok. After a brief visit at her home, complete with tea and biscuits, she thanked us, and then this eighty-year-old grandmother walked us up the hill to our truck to make sure we got out okay. It is funny because she was more concerned for us than we were.

When we got the opportunity to deliver a grandparent to the prison, it opened up a new world of ministry. Even though we spoke different languages and couldn't communicate as well, it still made a difference, and Christ still shone through and got the glory. Often, as Christians, our words just get in the way of our ministry intentions. So just step out in faith, show love, make the Jesus connection, and let God do the work. I always tell people that, in all my years, I know two certain facts in life: there is a Holy Spirit, and I'm not it.

So, during the car-buying experience and after a few days of searching and realizing the importance of a good reliable vehicle, we bought our first vehicle, a 1997 Toyota Surf 4x4. We parked it outside the door in our driveway. While looking out the window, we learned why we need to keep our front gate closed. Some local cattle wandered down the hill and camped out across the street from us. It was an awesome sight out our gate, and a good welcome to Uganda.

As we prepared for work next week, we prayed for safety and security for all the staff. We'd also had some time restrictions placed on the academy by the government for some code violations at the academy before they would certify us as a school. We all sat down and faced the list of wants and needs for Wells of Hope, as we looked over building plans and costs. We prayed that we'd all be good stewards of His finances and that they be multiplied. The effect Wells of Hope had on the community spread and affected not only prisoners and their children, but the village families as well. Praying for these families and sharing the good news with them was our mission.

One of the last things we needed to do during that second week in the country was to set up a local bank account, both for Uganda Shillings and US Dollars. The bank required a printed water bill to prove that we lived in the country. Because there were no house addresses or posted street names, the bill got dropped off at each person's door once a month, so it usually took a few months to get caught up. As Gina and I sat outside, doing our Bible study on Matthew the next day, the water guy walked up and handed us our water bill, saying we owe 3,743 Uganda Shillings (UGS) which is $1.40 USD. Praise God! God's perfect timing was on, and we were more confident than ever in our direction He had us on. But it only took a few days to hit our first downhill slide in our plan; thankfully, as always, God was steering.

Gina and I were able to get a lot of little things done that we needed to and learned a few hard lessons. We got pulled over again by the traffic police for turning right on red, which I guess is not allowed there. It was hard to tell because everyone else had turned, but we were the only ones stopped. He took us to traffic court. Traffic court turns out to be inside any Bank branch in town where you could fill out a form, pay the fine via your bank account, and get your license back.

My ticket was for careless driving, and those who live in Kampala are probably laughing out loud right now, because it is like driving in a zoo.

We drove by an accident between two trading centers on the way to the academy. The accident had just happened, and as we drove by slowly, it was easy to see that a motorcycle taxi (Boda Boda) was hit by a car, and one of the passengers was killed. I wanted to stop and check on them, but then saw a crowd running down the street from the trading center. We were informed by Mr. Ssuubi that they were not coming to check on them, but coming to watch, and some were even coming to steal the property of those injured or dead. Mr. Ssuubi told me also that in a traffic accident, someone can come up to you while you lay there on the ground, take your phone, call the police, then take out your SIM card and steal your phone while you watch. At least they called for help, I guess.

We continued to the trading center and informed a traffic officer of what happened. Mr. Ssuubi warned us that we should never stop for an accident but tell the police instead. If you stopped, they could sometimes blame you for it happening. Lesson learned, and that would come in handy in the near future.

As I mentioned before, it would not be long before we ran into our first downhill slide in Uganda life. I woke up one morning, seven days after buying the car, to put the kettle on to make some tea. I looked out of the kitchen window to see that the hood was up on the car. I first thought how strange that was, then thought that Eric, our newly hired "Security" guard, liked to wash the car every day. I thought, *"He must be out there."*

Then I looked down and realized the keys were on the kitchen table and the side mirrors on the truck were missing.

I was speechless. I felt violated and mad at the same time. Our car had been parked five feet from our front door! I wanted to call the police but realized there was nothing they could or would do. Someone had scaled an eight-foot wall, an iron gate, and razor wire. They had stolen the outside mirrors and window switches and had broken the door locks, starting to take the dashboard apart.

At this moment, I started feeling our vulnerability, and we started asking ourselves questions. What if they tried to get in the house? The police didn't respond, and Ugandan citizens weren't allowed to own guns. We were instructed if they tried to come back, to turn the lights on. If they tried to get in the house, we should make the sound of the Ugandan alarm system. The Ugandan alarm system is made by scraping a Panga (machete) across the concrete floor. This had the same effect as cocking a shotgun or pulling back the hammer on a .357

Magnum. No one stuck around to see if you'll use it.

During our time in Africa, we became friends with Sam Childers, of Machine Gun Preacher fame. Sam is a pastor and is famous for taking up arms against a rebel named Joseph Kony. Kony and his Lord's Resistance Army or LRA were famous for attacking villages in the Uganda, Sudan, and Congo regions. He would kill the parents and take the children to be soldiers in his attacks against other villages and government troops. Sam would go in and ambush Kony and his men to rescue these children and return them to a family member, or he would take them to one of his orphanages where he houses hundreds of children. They made a movie about Sam's life called *"Machine Gun Preacher."* Sam had lived in Uganda for many years and knew all about security. He told me that you could use Morten's roach spray as mace if they got close enough, but of course Sam was the Machine Gun Preacher and had a larger-than-life presence.

Things we depend on in our daily lives for security we take for granted. Some of these things are so little that we never think twice about it. Back in the US, I take comfort in the fact that if my elderly father became sick, my mother would call an ambulance. The ambulance would arrive, treat him, and take him to the hospital for care. If an accident happened and another car struck us, a traffic officer would respond in minutes. He would then take action to correct the situation in a fair and logical manner, and someone would be held responsible. Our homes are secure, and we have the right to bear arms as gun owners. If someone did break in, you'd call the police, and they'd respond in minutes to the scene to protect and serve; I've always believed that and still do to this day. Some of my best friends are policemen and EMT's, men and women driven to do the best job and serve the community they are in. Some people in America may think the police are crooked, or that medical responses are poor, but they have no idea how far off they are and how good they have it.

In hindsight, after the car was broken into that morning, it could have been a lot worse. David, the security guard for the house above us on the hill had heard them breaking into the car, looked down, and scared them off. He told us they would strip a car down to the metal around there. We started locking the Toyota in the garage every night and locking all the doors for security. We also bought a local dog and named her Molly. Most Africans were terrified of dogs, and she barked at pretty much everyone.

There's something about having that help just a phone call away that makes us feel confident. Someone you can depend on when things go wrong. This was the first time Gina and I had to move the boundaries of our comfort zones, and it would not be the last time. Making it through this first speed bump on our trip was a learning experience. When that confidence of men's protection is no longer there, how far are you willing to go? How vulnerable will you allow God to make you? The transition from worldly protection to spiritual protection had begun. You will never know how far you can go until you allow God to take you there. I was told once by my cousin Kim, "Life begins at the end of your comfort zone." At the end of your comfort zone is when you are tested and allow yourself to grow in spiritual strength and Godly dependency. As the military saying goes, "It's where the rubber meets the road. It's where the metal meets the meat."

CONTEXT AND PRETEXT

When we first came to work with Wells of Hope Ministries, we had envisioned ourselves working at the academy with the children most of the time. One of the great mysteries of living in Uganda was the elusive work permit. Many missionaries had been there for years, paying the monthly fees and going from three-month visa to three-month visa. They paid lots of money but never actually saw a work permit. It always took many trips to the immigration office and quite a few "fees" to find your file, but it didn't guarantee you would get a work permit. With the help of Janet at our office and the sheer grace of God, we received ours in three months, and Gina and I never set foot in a line. We were approved to live in Uganda for two years, and it was stamped by God.

Before we settled in with our jobs at the academy, we wanted to learn all the phases of the ministry, from the prison ministry to tracing to the academy life with the kids. The ministry really started to take off at the prison, and if you would have told me a year before that we would be the leaders of a prison ministry in Uganda, I would have thought you needed to have your head examined. God was changing our direction and attitudes on where we were going, and that was okay. As we began to teach in the prisons, we started with the four Gospels and went from the birth of John the Baptist to the resurrection of Jesus in order. We wanted to get back to the basics of God's Word, no more skipping around or pulling verses together to form a teaching topic. We started from the beginning to discuss in depth each verse and how it led to the next.

Take a book off a shelf, any book, open it to any page, and read one paragraph. No doubt you would learn a little something about the characters, the story, or even the plot, but overall, what could you learn? You could speculate, add some of your own details from personal experience, and fill in the rest to maybe make it seem logical. How much did you understand about the story, characters, history, and reasoning of those involved? Do we truly understand the morale of the story from just a paragraph?

There's something about studying the Word of God in order that gives us a deeper understanding of what he means and how things were. We miss key lessons when we just cherry pick verses and not do a whole word study, combining them to see the big picture. When we pick and choose Scripture too often, we fill in the blanks with our own ignorance.

The most difficult thing to do in a Ugandan prison was to explain things in a Bible study without using descriptions they wouldn't understand. For example, when we talked about a Scripture, I would have to illustrate local places, people, or cultural references to make sense. To explain the story of Matthew and God's grace, I would explain Matthew was a tax collector or publican in some translations. He collected money that was not his and gave the impression that the people had no choice, which made him very disliked among his fellow Jews. Some of the inmates may have understood half of that, but they did not truly understand the level of despising the Jewish people had for Matthew. So, I would explain to them that Matthew was tax collector that took money from people that was not his, like a Ugandan Traffic Officer. They stop you for no reason, imply you broke the law, even though in most cases you did nothing wrong, and they would make you bribe them to let you go. It's called contextualization. Only then did the inmates understand the level of despising people had for Matthew, which in turn helped Ugandans better understand how much Jesus deeply loved Matthew, despite his sinfulness. To better understand love, you need to better understand hate.

To contextualize better, we really started to ask questions on things in Uganda. We needed to understand the people's attitudes, how they did things, and why. To better understand the Gospel and use their cultural references, we had to understand their culture better and teach better, and as a result we can disciple better.

We started to read more about culture, and Gina and I went to Wednesday night classes at our church being taught by African Center for Apologetics Research (ACFAR). ACFAR was the leading expert on cults and religious movements in the country and was offering an inside view of what the people believed. The first thing we noticed was that in Uganda, Jesus was all over everything. Jesus Christ Pharmacy, God is Able Taxi Service, Holy Spirit Hardware Store, etc. It was exciting to see everyone so spiritually motivated and Holy-Spirit filled. We started to wonder why we might even be there. But it didn't take long to see how shallow the roots really were, and it started to concern us. More than once, someone had told us that spiritually there it was an ocean wide but only an inch deep. We quickly found ourselves on the battlefield of a struggle between Christianity, Catholicism, Islam, witchcraft, and deep cultural roots. After looking at the big picture, it was clear that some of those lines were starting to get blurry and, in some cases, disappear completely. We wondered how it got to this point. I mean, Jesus was everywhere, all over everything.

Jesus was all around, and people knew His name and who He was. During our Bible study, we were pleased to see that many of the men and women had a very good working knowledge of God and His word, and the study seemed to take off quickly. But questions soon began to rise that made us scratch our heads. Gina would pass around a prayer book on each visit to the prison and ask each inmate to write down a prayer request they had or something that was on their minds we could pray for. By far, without a doubt, the most popular prayer request was to be released from prison. Then for God to forgive their sins, for God to heal them, and for God to bless them abundantly. One after another, they would ask Gina and me to pray for the forgiveness of their sins and for God to bless them abundantly. The first request seemed very easy to take on and discuss. I first asked how many there needed prayers for the forgiveness of their sins, and most of the hands went up in the room. How many needed prayers for healing? Again, most of the hands went up. I then asked how many of them have prayed these things for themselves. With that, there was not much of a response from the group. I then closed my lesson plan on Matthew and made a change to the plan, going to another lesson on asking God to forgive you, which means coming from a true heart of repentance. It is about a relationship with God, just you and Him. There is no salesman, no priest, no rabbi, no pastor, no witch doctor, no bribery fees; it is just you and Jesus. Period.

1 TIMOTHY 2:5
There is one God and one mediator between God and men, the man Christ Jesus.

The curtain was torn from top to bottom, and it was finished by our Lord and Savior, Jesus Christ. Through Him, and only through Him, are we saved.

We now understood that everyone we met had heard His name and knew who Jesus was but didn't have a relationship with Him. A believer that's not rooted in God's word is a tree that can be blown over easily when the first storm of life comes along, because the roots are not firm. Somehow the introduction to Jesus was made, but there was no follow up, no nurturing, and no growth. There was no discipleship, just knowledge. Were people only sharing the Gospel and nothing else?

The Gospel or Good News of Jesus Christ is written into four books, Matthew, Mark, Luke, and John. These are the direct accounts of our

Lord and Savior, His teaching in His words when He was on this planet. He teaches us everything we need to know about the kingdom and its coming. I often wondered why it took four books to deliver His message but took twenty-one books to provide us with follow up, corrective direction, admonishment, and sometimes even praise.

So, in theory, roughly fifteen percent of the New Testament is the Gospel of Jesus, and the other eighty-five is follow up, teaching, corrective direction, and admonishment of the first fifteen percent. It's Paul, the disciples, and followers checking on progress of the churches and fellowships they started. They were following up with the other believers around the area and providing discipleship opportunity. They spent time traveling around great distances to encourage Christian communities and provide correction and direction. Are we now doing fifteen percent of the work and missing the nurturing and follow up that Paul and the disciples did in the other eighty-five percent of the New Testament?

Was this lack of Scripture study and deeper understanding causing so many problems and the reason why the roots of believers were so shallow? Was this why so many believers were moving from church to church, or leaving the church all together? Was this why so many were taking parts of the Gospel and blending it with other religious practices, forming their own groups? As disciples of Christ, how many of us were doing the return trips to our roots to nurture the new believers, going out of our way to encourage them in their growth and provide spiritual direction through the continued reading of His Word? All these things needed to be addressed by getting back to the basics of one-on-one study.

Since our return to Uganda in January, we had focused on the prison ministry more because the children at the academy were all at their home villages on break for a month and a half. Armed with this new information on the importance of discipleship in Scripture, we made a prison-ministry plan that was less on just the knowledge of God, but more to get them to build a relationship with the relational God.

Outside the western world and Europe, community and relationships are vital to survival. This is a stark contrast with the western world's idea of being an individual. In the majority of the world, everyone knows you and you know everyone. Understanding this would be a challenge for Gina and me as westerners, because we would have to deal with the loss of our individual identity and embrace the group culture, but this change would be nothing compared to the speed bump we had lying directly ahead.

Lord, thank you for your daily protection. I pray that you help us to trust in you more and do away with our spirit of fear, and that the fear we have may not be a stumbling block to us. That we do not depend on the security of the world, but that you are our help and eternal security in times of trouble.

Chapter 9

THE EARLY HIGHS AND LOWS

"The only easy day, was yesterday"
-US Navy SEALS

ON OUR FIVE-WEEK VISION TRIP to Wells of Hope Uganda, we met a five-year-old girl named "Agnes," a child of God, and, in my eyes, a beautiful little princess. She was a student at the Wells of Hope Academy, the boarding school for children with a parent in prison. Agnes and her two older sisters, Rose, and Sarah were at the academy because both their father and mother were in prison, each serving sixty years. We never really asked why anyone was there because it changed nothing; all we needed to know was that they were broken and in need, just like anyone else.

We first met Agnes wearing a dress with a watermelon on it, and she was the cutest girl around. The youngest children would approach

200

Gina and I without hesitation or fear of us and always wanted to hold our hands. We realized quickly that Agnes was the poster child for Wells of Hope, and we understood why. Gina quickly formed a bond with Agnes, and she could frequently be seen as an accessory on Gina's lap.

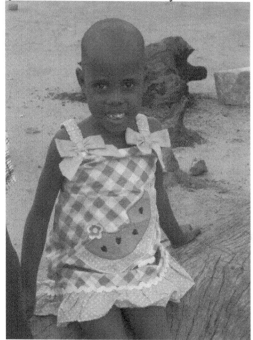

(Photo taken by Gina Gant)

After the five weeks, we went home to the US on a brief three-month break and did some fundraising, and Agnes was a focal point of our fundraising presentations. Agnes' family was the first of the academy families we were able to meet. Both parents were in prison for sixty years, and the grandmother took care of the children in the village before WOH got them. Because of this, we were able to form a close bond with the family on all levels, and it made it very real for us. When we returned to Uganda three months later to start our first year, it was quiet at the school because mostly all the children were home on one of their three-term breaks to spend time with their families in the village.

The first few weeks had been a blessing, and, besides the car being broken into, the transition was seamless. We were getting settled in, doing work at the office, and focusing on the prison ministry. The day finally arrived, and the children were all on their way back to the office to be bused back to the academy to start a new school term. We had a visitor at the office, doing a presentation on prisons in the UK as we all waited for the children's return. Some children had already made it back and were waiting patiently in the grass area in front of the office.

During the presentation, the office had received a phone call that Agnes was not feeling well, and the transport wanted to take her by the doctor instead of coming straight to the office, and it was approved. During our next break in the presentation, I was pulled aside and told that Agnes had died in the van on the way to the office. I was stunned. We told no one until after the presentation was over for fear of disrupting our guest.

At that point I could not think of anything but her face and thought I might cry. I kept looking over at Gina during the rest of the presentation, and I knew she would be devastated at this news, so we waited until the time was right to tell everyone.

We mourned the loss of that little girl. It struck everyone hard, and she would be greatly missed. She was someone we had come to know and love very much. We never realized that, when we flew home three months earlier, it would be the last time we would ever see her again. Agnes was believed to have died from complications of a disease known as sickle cell anemia, an inherited red blood cell disorder in which there aren't enough healthy red blood cells to carry oxygen throughout your body.

Normally, the flexible, round red blood cells move easily through blood vessels. In sickle cell anemia, the red blood cells are shaped like sickles or crescent moons. These rigid, sticky cells can get stuck in small blood vessels, which can slow or block blood flow and oxygen to parts of the body. There's no cure for most people with sickle cell anemia but treatments which are relatively easy to give and do not cost very much, can relieve pain, and help prevent complications associated with the disease.[1] What happened was a simple

---

[1] https://www.mayoclinic.org/diseases-conditions/sickle-cell-anemia/symptoms-causes/syc-20355876

case of being forgetful. The children were home on break and the grandmother had lapsed on giving her the medication until it was too late.

Agnes had died from a disease that was passed on to her genetically and she had no control over it. She was loved and will be missed by all that knew her. We mourn for those we know, love and have lost.

Think about all the death that goes on around the world, I mean needless death. Death here in Africa is very real and daily. From natural events to accidents and simple sickness that could have been prevented by $2 medicine. In my home in Jacksonville, I put the number "25,000" on my refrigerator door for my kids to see every day. In the book by Richard Stearns entitled, "The Hole in our Gospel," I learned that globally 25,000 children die every day from lack of food, water, and medicine. I wanted my kids to never forget that statistic as they went to the refrigerator to get a glass of clean water or the make themselves something to eat. On the day Agnes died, that number 25,000 got a face.

UNDERSTANDING THE MEANING OF LOSS

Stories of loss started to become very common in our ministry travels. Sometimes all you could do was just listen. When we visited men and women in prison, we got a chance to hear their testimonies, and sometimes they were so heart moving and gut wrenching to hear at the same time. How some of these inmates had been in prison for three or four years and had not even been to court yet. Most had lost everything, job, house, family, children, and wife, all gone. Some just were in the wrong place at the wrong time.

During prayer time with them, we asked them what we could pray about with them, and by far most wanted to know why they were in prison. Not for the reason of crime, but many began to ask what God's purpose for them being in prison was. They said things like, "I've always tried to be a good person," or "I do good things for people. I go to church, and I pray louder than anyone. Why has God brought me to prison and taken everything away?" So, we encouraged them to not pray for outright release from prison, but more importantly, for God's will to be fulfilled in their lives. That they pray for their time in prison to be led by God and, when they were ready, to be released on God's time to be followers of Him.

Many prisoners would admit that they lived their own lives on their own terms, and that's what brought them here today. We encouraged them to take advantage of the short time they had in prison and to talk to God and spend quality time studying His Word. We liked to call their time in prison "Discipleship University." This was not only a time for salvation awaking, because many may have already known Him, but a spiritual awaking. They needed to admit that they couldn't do it on their own, they needed God.

During one lesson, we talked about "Blessed are those that are poor in spirit." We were not talking about being poor as in having no money or possessions, but we were still talking about a spiritual need, a hunger so deep that it is a good thing. When our lives seem full of the world, and it becomes a distraction, we no longer depend on God. Our calendars are full of cool things that keep us busy and make us feel like we are living a comfortable life because we avoid anything that will make us uncomfortable or resembles suffering. But we are spiritually dead inside, nailing our coffins shut using the business of life.

Author C.S. Lewis explains it this way, "I'm not sure God wants us to be happy, I think he wants us to love and be loved. But we are like children thinking our toys will make us happy and the whole world is our nursery. Something must drive us out of that nursery and into the lives of others, and that something is suffering."

Some of us do not even realize how spiritually dead we are inside, and that should scare believers. What are we depending on? Man? Works? Things?

God wants us to be 100% spiritually dependent on Him, because He is the sole provider that matters. When our life is too cluttered, and we no longer depend on Him, He sometimes takes those things away to get our attention. It may seem bad at first, but like a loving father, He knows what is best for us. The best place a worldly rich man can be is spiritually broken, with all distractions removed. Men and women who find themselves unable to cope with life on their own are on their knees, looking to God. Glorious is the moment when we cross the boundary of the low point in our life and realize we cannot do it on our own. The junk food of our lives is gone; we are hungry again. We are hungry for God.

Some will try to attain salvation through good works and good deeds, but it's all empty without God's saving grace in our lives. You might be the best volunteer around, but you can still be dead in spirit.

The sad fact is that there are millions of people in the world today that have crossed their spiritual low point. Instead of turning to God, their hearts have become so hard that they just get a shovel and dig a new low point in their life. They continue to set new lows that will define who they are in themselves and not in God. Believe me, I know. They say things like "I'll show the world that I am strong. I will never quit because I am powerful!" They try to build on their own strength when all they do is get weaker, more fragile, and continue to break God's heart for them.

Someone who is poor in spirit realizes that he is unable to provide for himself spiritually. He depends completely on God for his salvation. He knows that all the good works he can scrounge up will not be nearly enough to pay his debts. He trusts in God alone. The awareness of an impoverished spirit leads to realization. Realization leads to repentance. Repentance leads to spiritual awakening. Spiritual awakening leads to a fulfilled life. Welcome back from the dead, my friend.... welcome back.

KEEPING THE TANK FULL

The hard part of ministry is you can sometimes run low on your compassion tank. It can get hard to love those people who hit their low point especially when it happens repeatedly.

One day, we had some visitors from the USA, Todd, and Cindy Lemmon, who were staying with us for a few days before they flew back to the United States. Todd was a retired police officer from Jacksonville, and they were here to investigate ministry opportunities in Uganda. His plan was to retire from the Jacksonville Sheriff's Office (JSO), go to nursing school, and return to Uganda to operate a medical clinic in the country. Although we had never met before, we shared a mutual friend, Terri Terrell from our church in Jacksonville, who served with Todd at JSO. Terri told the Lemmon's about Gina and I and said if we were in Kampala, that maybe we should meet for dinner or something. It's funny now, but the

Lemmon's, who were strangers when we met in Uganda, became some of our closest friends and prayer supporters, and in Jacksonville, we lived less than a mile from each other.

While they were with us, we received a call from our director, Francis Ssuubi. He informed us that there was a case at the police station that we all needed to investigate. Gina and I had been in the prisons many times and knew most of the staff, so we were comfortable in these situations. When this case came up at the Kawempe police station in Kampala, I thought it would be interesting for Todd, being a retired cop, to get an inside look at a Uganda Police station, so we all went together.

At the station, we were introduced to a young man around ten years old named Willie. He was visibly scared and had been crying. We were brought in a room with tables, chairs, and a couch. They soon brought in a man named Patrick, who was directed to sit on the couch in front of us. Every police station had family units to deal with domestic issues and child abandonment cases, which is why they sometimes called Wells of Hope. The police officer, who informed us that Patrick was believed to be Willie's father, began to question Patrick. The officer also told us that Patrick had been caught in a police sting operation, trying to sell his son to a man that would use him for a child sacrifice.

Child sacrifice is not uncommon and is a serious problem. Child sacrifice still happens and is even blended into religious practice in some parts of the villages. Some proclaiming Christians still participate in such acts like witchcraft because it's so engrained into their culture in the deep villages. They treat witchcraft like a fallback plan, "Just in case this Jesus thing doesn't work out."

I also learned about this type of cultural viewpoint when I studied the 1994 genocide in Rwanda that took the lives of one million people in a period of hundred days. While investigating the collapse of church beliefs in Rwanda, A Vatican priest asked why a country that was 85% Christian would turn on each other and commit such atrocities? The response by some of the local Rwandan church leadership was, "Tribal blood is deeper than baptismal waters."[22]

Another time, Gina and I drove through a remote village in the Northeast, and a sign at the roundabout read, "Say no to child sacrifice." It still gives me chills today that they would have to remind people that children should not be killed for their gods. To prevent some children from being taken or sold, the parents pierced the ears of the child. The skull loses power if the ears are pierced because the value is in the head.

---

[2] Emmanuel Katongole, "Mirror to the church: Resurrecting Faith after Genocide in Rwanda" p.22,

As we sat in that police station, I felt sick for Patrick and mad at the same time. How could you sell your own flesh and blood to be used for a sacrifice by some witch doctor? The story was that he brought his son to Kampala from Kenya and was approached about the sale. Patrick believed he could sell Willie and use the money to start a new life with land, a house, and a new wife. Some questions began to arise if he was even the boy's father. The confusion happens often in the culture because it is not uncommon for a boy to call his male caretaker "Father" out of respect.

To imagine him being the real father made me sick, and I could not understand how a father could do this to his own child. Who would care to be around a man that would sell his own son? In situations like these, so many men like Patrick just disappeared into the legal system and were never seen or heard from again, and I was okay with that. It was early on in our time in Uganda and my compassion tank was already becoming depleted.

The Wells of Hope team took the boy Willie to the academy and got him settled in, and he started to take classes and make friends. A few months went by, and we continued to try to communicate with Willie and get him comfortable in his new surroundings. He did not speak English or Luganda but was making progress in classes. He had not been told about what his father had done, and we all agreed that it should stay that way.

UNDERSTANDING MEEKNESS AND WEAKNESS

Driving in Uganda was a tough lesson for me on many levels. I know it may sound simple or silly, like how hard can it be to adjust to driving? But it was quite a complex problem for me. To learn the rules of the road would not take long and would come easily, but that was not the problem. I was a strong-willed person, and in Uganda, I had to face one of my biggest pet peeves. I did not like it when people thought they were better than others—not just better than me, but mostly other people. The ones that openly, purposely, and deliberately took advantage of the weak and feeble minded.

There were two types of drivers here, offensive, and defensive. Offensive drivers drove aggressively, asserting their will, passing without caution, and constantly endangering others around them. They were the people driving on the sidewalks, purposely pulling out in front of people so they will stop for them. As a new driver here, you had to go into survival mode and adapt to the driving style to survive. You became one of them. We had seen and heard of Mzungus (Ma-Zoon-Goos), which is Luganda for white people, that had conformed to the aggressive, take, take, take style of driving there. I was all about love, order, discipline—stand in line and wait your turn. Here there were no lines or waiting of any kind. The aggressive took advantage of the weaker, and I hated to consider myself weak.

The "world" defines strong people as those who are assertive, take charge, proud, self-sufficient, self-reliant, self-motivated, and independent. All these things listed in the world's "strong category" seem to lean toward vain attitudes and self-dependence.

A meek person is the opposite of these things. A meek person is willing to be submissive, is humble and gentle, relies on God, and is dependent on God to provide strength. There is no "self" listed in meekness. So many people associate meekness with weakness, but there is a difference.

Weakness is defined as lack of strength, determination, or lack of ability; a weak point in the structure or arrangement of something. A character flaw which can be a feature of somebody's character regarded as unfavorable. Any follower that is God's definition of meekness will never fall into this category. First, we draw our strength from the Lord, so we will never lack strength. Secondly, we cannot lack ability because each one of us has God-given abilities and gifts that we recognize. Thirdly and most important, we all admit we have character flaws, and God loves us despite our shortcomings because we realize His grace is enough. So, no follower of God can be weak; it is fundamentally impossible. After studying all this, here is what I came up with. A "strong" man who tries to stand on his own may seem strong to the world, but in reality, he is weak. His life is filled with hollow self-centered dreams and shallow relationships. This is all proved by the attributes he has. The only ability he has is being assertive; he must dominate situations and control others by asserting himself and his will, just to get the sense of success that he covets. His actions cause so-called "friends" to surround him. He also tries to control them because deep down inside he trusts only himself to do anything. In the end, this makes him lonely because he trusts no one and shallow because he has no idea what a true relationship is. If this is how the world defines a strong person, I want no part of it.

One day, after four different cars rubbed up against me in the same day in traffic, I was at the point of exploding on the next person that drove into me. When it came to driving, I could easily adapt to my driving surroundings and be the strong and assertive type, or I could try to drive the best I could, use compassion, and do the right thing by being gracious, passive and forgiving. I chose to control myself; I chose to be meek.

So, what is the difference between a strong and meek person? What makes a person of meekness? Meekness is a person's ability to recognize that he carries inside him the world's definition of strength, but, through the Holy Spirit, he controls it and does not allow it to take over. Anyone can take, take, and take, but few can control it, submit, and give. Now that takes strength, and that is meekness.

A MESSAGE FROM THE LORD

One day, as I drove to the Upper Prison at Luzira, we were scheduled to do our Four Gospel Discipleship Study that day, both spending two and a half hours in Boma and two and a half hours in the condemned, death row section. During the time we visited the men and women in prison, we kept track of who attended the course and conducted a graduation at the end with certificates for completion. We wanted to get each one of the inmates a Bible during the course, so they could follow along instead of giving them a Bible at the end as a reward. But we were warned that we should not just give Bibles away because some of the inmates would take one and use it for other things rather than reading it, like smoking or toilet paper.

We told them, if they wanted to misuse the Word of God, they would have to answer to someone much higher than us. But we would not stand before that same God and explain why we kept the Word of God from them because of what they might do. Because of free will, life is full of choices, and I will always present the choices and allow them to choose and deal with the consequences and God.

As I drove that day, Gina read me the daily situation reports for the country and got caught up on emails. One email message that morning left us feeling heavy hearted and took the wind right out of us. We had been holding onto the hope that my girls, Ashton, and Gabby, would be able to come out to see us in Uganda and see what we do for the Lord. The email said that their mom believed it was too dangerous for them to travel to Uganda. Accompanied or not, she was saying no to them ever coming out to see us where we work. The rest of the day, I struggled through the five-plus hours of class, still thinking of what had happened, trying to understand it. We wanted so badly to share with them everything we were doing in ministry. We could never have felt more isolated than that day. Teaching that day kept my mind occupied, but the moment I stopped, I would remember and be depressed.

The topic was Jesus' Baptism and immediate temptation—how, while the Spirit led Jesus into the wilderness, He did not send Him alone; the Spirit was with Him. When we receive the Holy Spirit as Christians, we have this sense of invulnerability, but the truth is Jesus tells us to be careful of our pride. Life will not be perfect, we will be tempted, and we will walk in the wilderness. We just need to ask ourselves whether we are being led by the Spirit or is our pride leading us.

That day, we were in our wilderness but surrounded by people. As usual, over a hundred inmates wanted to talk to us afterwards, but there was just not enough time. Normally the inmate pastor helped us through the crowd, to the gate before too many people crowded around and made it impassable. But after this second teaching session, a leader of the inmate church group named Alex brought an elderly man to us, who said he had something very important he had to tell us. Like the parting of the sea, the crowd moved, and the old man approached us. Recognizing the importance of the situation, we sat back down and listened to him.

Through a translator, the old man then said, "I was told three separate times that I must talk to you. Pastor Steve, you and your wife pass around your prayer request book every time you are here, you care, and your people back home pray for us daily." Then out of the blue he asked us, "How many children do you have?"

I responded, "We have two."

He then said, "I need to know how I am supposed to pray for you and them."

He was told to pray for us! I broke down and told him about the message we had received just that morning about the hopes of our children visiting being canceled and how heavy our hearts were at that moment. He then prayed over us,

217

and I never saw him again. Though the girls were never able to come see us, at that moment a peace came over us like a tidal wave. Gina and I both knew this was out of our hands; we turned everything over to God, and He was telling us that He was with us.

A few months later, Gina and I were at Boma Upper Prison. We had just finished a Bible study and were walking to the gate to leave. The usual crowds of inmates who wanted to shake hands and talk followed us. As we passed through the group that numbered around a thousand, a man approached me and asked if I remembered him.

Now we got approached a lot and asked for many requests, but this one was different. I took my concentration from the person I was talking too, and I stared at the man for a minute. He looked familiar somehow, but I could not place him, and it was hard to concentrate with all the noise. All at once, his face came into focus, and I could see that the man was Patrick, Willie's father. The man that had tried to sell his son for a child sacrifice. I remembered how I'd thought when they took Patrick away months before that I would probably never see him again and how I was okay with that. In the prison system men disappear all the time and are never heard from, often dying alone in a cell. That day, I asked myself the same questions I asked before. Who would want to be around a man that would sell his own son? Who could love a man like that?

Who could have compassion for a man like that? The answer was that Jesus would, and that day I decided so would I. The man I once thought they should lock up and throw away the key, I now saw in a different light. I saw his face and the brokenness that he lived in. I saw a man that Jesus loved. At that moment, I was so excited to see him. I just reached out and hugged him like he was a long-lost brother, patting him hard on the back, like most Americans do. With a clear look of shock on his face, he told me, "Pastor, things are not good here." I just smiled in return and looked him right in the face and replied, "I know Patrick, you're in prison!"

I realized that God had brought him back across my path for a reason. God was softening my heart for sinners, even those I considered the worst of the worst. God was telling me, "Remember this guy you cast judgement on? I love you and him too." I was just happy to see Patrick and know that he was alive. I felt like I had another chance in a situation I failed at before. Everything Patrick had done before was forgotten, and all I could see was his face. The face of a man that I know God loved and just like me, was working on.

Lord, mend our hearts in times of loss. Help us to mourn in a healthy way that honors you. That our loss will not become an obstacle in our walk, but a motivation. Continue to turn the soil of our hearts and break our hearts for what breaks yours to draw us to those that need to hear about you. Thank you for the gift of grace and mercy for others as you have given it to us.

Chapter 10

THE WHOLE TRUTH AND NOTHING BUT THE TRUTH

Study to shew thyself approved unto God, a workman that needeth not to be ashamed, rightly dividing the word of truth.

2 Timothy 2:15

THE PRISON MINISTRY Bible study continued to go verse by verse, and this in-depth way of reading had brought us even closer to our Bible study battle cry: "Don't take my word for it, read it for yourself."

I told inmates, "When I walk out these gates, I want you to search the Scripture and read it over and over and over again."

So many people go to church, listen to the pastor, nod their heads, throw in a few "Amens" for good measure, and go home. This may seem like an okay practice for some, but in an African society that preys on the uneducated and poor, and that is not good.

1 Thessalonians 5:21 says, *"Prove all things, hold fast that which is good."*

We encouraged the prisoners, "When someone tells you something from the Bible, read it for yourself and prove it. You are not doing this to be difficult or hardheaded, but to stand firm in the truth. With every passing moment, and every Scripture you study, your roots will grow deeper and deeper. Be very careful of a pastor that preaches from the Bible and never opens it up. Be cautious of what we call the 'one-verse theologian' who can talk for hours, shouting on one verse. I am not saying it's all bad but use the opportunity to study it for yourself."

There are so many local religious groups in Uganda that "poach" Christians who are weak in the word. They see that the new convert is not sure about his beliefs yet and, like a young animal, is excited about the new world he lives in. He is hungry and reckless. He is the one who is usually the most eager and excited, and through his lack of discernment, our new creature in Christ breaks away from the herd. The poachers then pull out their little pamphlets and "Bible companion books" and show him how their group's beliefs are true. They even make it seem like it is part of the Bible itself. They show them how it goes right along with certain Scriptures that were chosen from the Word of God. Of course, they sound like they go together; they handpicked the Scripture, took it out of context, then wrote their own version of it. Of course, they believe in it because they wrote it.

True believers that stand firm in the Word will not be easily swayed or stray from the group. When someone falls behind, they are easily picked off by the predators. As part of the herd, we must also pay better attention to the small ones that start to wander off. Especially when they're being overzealous and irritating everyone around them.

One such time happened on a visitation to the northwest corner of Uganda, on the border of the Democratic Republic of the Congo and South Sudan in a small city called Aura. We had been driving from Mbale on the eastern border and making our way across the country to the western border. Over a four-day period, we visited families and traced missing children for Wells of Hope. Before we left for our trip, our American friend Emily had given us a book to give to a local Ugandan named Moses, who she had met sometime before and still lived in Aura. We figured if we were already in the area and our schedule permitted, it would be okay.

We stopped for the night in a small town called Pachwach just across the Nile River. We had a late dinner in one of the local restaurants and ate the little food they had left over. Having an adventurous palate, I was up for trying anything and ate the last serving of the local millet they had. I remember picking gravel out of the food, and the taste was something I will never forget. It was spicy, which I am sure it should not have been, but by the light of the one bulb in the room I could barely see it, which I thought was for the best.

They shut down the power in the town for the night as Gina and I settled into our tin hut. I recall rolling over in the night from my back and feeling the puddle of sweat run off my chest and down to the cot.

I informed Gina that I had not slept well and had lost a lot of fluids the night before. That morning after tea and bread, we hit the road and, as we approached Aura, I had this sense that I needed to throw up, and I did right there on the side of the road. Assuming I was just dehydrated, we continued with our work and picked up an ex-inmate named Richard Odong that we were planning to visit and see how he was after being released. With his release from prison, Richard's children had left the academy and were back to living with him in Aura. Richard had attended our Bible studies in the prison, and it was good to see him on the outside doing well. This was the first time we had a person released from prison, and we wanted to see how well the reunion with his children was going. We visited his home, and all crowded into the small straw thatch hut, all sweating with no air movement. I still felt terrible, and as we talked, all I could think about was getting out of that hut. I stared at the opening, and, when they started to pray, I saw my chance and I went outside.

The fresh air felt good on my face as I walked around the yard. I walked toward a tree to steady myself when things started to flicker black, like a switch off and on. I remember saying to myself, "God, I don't want to die," and that was the last thing I remembered.

I woke up, my face hurting from hitting the ground and my glasses crooked. I had no idea how long I had been there, but I sat up and tried to figure out where I was. Gina and the family we were visiting came out to see me sitting on the ground under an avocado tree with dirt on my face.

Normally after the visit we would have started the ten-hour drive home to Kampala, but after about an hour of gathering my strength, I got up, and we decided to try to get me to a doctor. Instead of parting ways with Richard Odong, he offered to guide us to a good doctor in town.

The doctor's office was more like an old defunct concrete building in a trading center in Aura. As we walked in, we had to wait because they were wheeling out an old woman who had just died, and this did not boost my confidence in the doctor.

After testing my blood, they told me I had malaria and a bacterial infection and needed three treatments over three days. We decided it was best to stay another night instead of trying to drive the ten hours back to Kampala. Getting IV's and the first two malaria treatments, I lay on the mattress, just trying to get my strength back. Sitting next to the bed was Gina, our friend Richard who graciously stayed with us and our travel companions Mariam and Stella from the Wells of Hope office.

While I recovered, Gina decided it would be a good time to call Emily's Ugandan friend Moses and give him the book Emily wanted us to deliver to him. Moses came in soon, greeted us, and Gina gave him the book. After we visited for a while, Moses got up to say his goodbyes and walked out.

For a long time, Moses and Richard stood just outside the door of my room, in what seemed to be in a heated discussion over something in their native language. It seemed that they knew each other. Eventually someone explained to us what had happened, and it all became clear what God was doing in this situation.

It turns out that the book we were bringing to Moses in Aura was about a cult called The Message Church, founded by a so-called prophet named William Branham. Emily had grown up in The Message Church in the US and left the cult. Years later, she lived in northern Uganda where

The Message Church and William Branham were very popular and met Moses, who had also left the cult. It turns out that Moses knew Richard, who was still in The Message Church cult. Moses confronted Richard right outside my door about the heresy that was The Message. If I had not gotten sick, Richard and I would have parted ways and I would have left thinking Richard was on the path he needed to be on. Never did I dream that he would have strayed that far. Everything Moses had said and done seemed to say he was on track with the Lord, but underneath we found out that he had fallen behind the pack and had gotten picked off by a lie perpetrated by self-proclaimed prophet William Branham.

This made us really think through our approach to discipleship. Our concern was that followers were wandering off the path and being taken away. Were we failing our new believers? Were we leaving them on their own too early to be snatched away?

We are not the only religion that sends out missionaries. Muslims too are feeding the hungry and clothing the naked. In Africa and much of the world, Islam builds schools, healthcare centers, and mosques for worship. Believers who lack a basic understanding of the Gospel are going where the rice is being handed out and school fees are paid for. Only if you follow Islam, kneel beside them at the mosque, and pray to Allah will you get the material help. The Great Commission says, "Go ye therefore, and teach all nations, baptizing them in the name of the Father, the Son and the Holy Spirit, teaching them to observe all things whatsoever I have commanded you. Teaching them the word of God and the truth to stand firm on." We need to pay more attention to phase two of the Great Commission, teaching.

On some foreign mission fields, we are converting at a record pace and spending less time teaching long term at the local level. The teaching cannot be done in an afternoon or a passing conversation, it takes time and dedication. This is what discipleship is and what Jesus Himself did. He chose men and taught them.

Past success has been measured in the baptism tally when they declare their faith publicly. Then, when they are still young and vulnerable, they get separated from the heard and are easily picked off. Our fellow believers deserve better from us, and God commands us to keep working.

Working in the prison system in Uganda, we have seen so many of the "new creatures" who were led astray by half-truths, blurring of the lines, and outright lies. The prison is like a fenced-in pen that holds the lost lambs. It is a place where many of the men find themselves face to face with God. Some will embrace this opportunity, relish in it, and become washed new. But some will continue to run and hide from His face, like scared little children hiding behind a mask of manhood.

Some men will hear the call and answer it while in the prison. We became friends with many of these inmates, like Pastor Peter in condemned prison, Pastors Mark, and Joshua in Murchison Bay Prison, Pastor Alex in Boma General, and Pastor Susan in Luzira women's prison. These men and women were hungry for the Word and were responsible for anywhere from 100 to 3,000 fellow inmate's spiritual needs. Through the donations to Gant Missions Uganda, we were able to provide them with cases of Bibles, books, pens, soap, and hygiene items, and we were able to be a small part of God's long-term discipleship plan in that country. The prison churches' focus was to study God's word and speak in Spirit and truth.

It is the believer's drive to hunger and thirst for righteousness that can only be found in God. But are they ready? Are they able to tell the good food from the junk?

ACTS 17:11 KJV
"These were more noble than those in Thessalonica, in that they received the word with all readiness of mind, and searched the scriptures daily, whether those things were so"

In the book of Acts, at the beginnings of the church, Paul was praising the new believers who were ready to receive the Word. Not only were they excited, but they prepared their minds for the Scripture. They listened to the Word, and, most importantly, they searched the Scriptures every day to check the facts they were told. This type of study made it hard for a believer to easily be led astray from the narrow path of God. It gave the sheep the ability to know the Shepherd's voice.

What does it mean to be ready in your mind, to thirst and hunger? Look at the overview of the Gospels of Jesus, and you'll notice there are always three main people groups in almost every story.

1) Jesus
2) His disciples and followers
3) Pharisees, Sadducees

When Jesus was teaching, He was usually followed by His disciples and followers but also by the Pharisees and Sadducees. Both groups got the same message, they listened to the same words Jesus spoke, they heard the same parables Jesus taught. So why did some believe and others not? Miracles, healings, and teachings were done, and some would dance in the streets and share with others on what they had seen, while the other group plotted to kill Jesus based on the same information.

Numerous times, Jesus taught the crowds and referenced Old Testament Scripture. So why didn't the Pharisees and Sadducees look it up for themselves? Why didn't they search the Scriptures to see and believe? Because they were not ready in their minds. They were not searching for answers, because they believed that they had the answer already. They were no longer hungry, they were no longer thirsty, because they were already full. They were full of self-righteousness.

These men who were full no longer searched to be fed. They knew all the rules because they wrote them. The Pharisees and Sadducees had polluted the Word of God so much, that they believed in their own importance, power, and righteousness, they were filled and no longer hungry.

The opposite was true about men who were searching for someone to believe in, someone to deliver them. They were hungry for a savior, and that man was the promised Messiah, Jesus Christ. He was the one they had been waiting for. They were hungry and thirsty and ready for Him. They searched, they heard, they saw, they believed.

Men that hunger and thirst for righteousness also need to understand what righteousness in God is. It is not seeking self-righteousness, but it is the righteousness that comes from God. It is to not depend on our own willpower to achieve it but to depend upon God. In Jesus' time, if there was anybody who would seem to qualify for such earnest passion, righteousness, and zeal for God, it would be the Pharisees and the Scribes (teachers of the Law).

But in the same chapter (Matthew 5:20), Jesus made a startling statement that would have had every man reeling. "For I tell you that unless your righteousness surpasses that of the Pharisees and the teachers of the Law, you will certainly not enter the kingdom of heaven."

The people must have thought, "How can this be done? There is no chance for us!" The Pharisees and Sadducees were seen as the most righteous of them all.

What kind of righteousness was Jesus talking about? Romans 3:21-22 answers the question. "But now righteousness of God apart from the Law is revealed, being witnessed by the Law and the Prophets, even the righteousness of God through faith in Jesus Christ, to all and on all who will believe."

So then, righteousness of God is available through faith in Jesus Christ to all who believe in Him. And those who will seek Him will find Him and will be filled. Jesus Himself claimed to be the one who would quench the thirst of those that are thirsty: "If any man thirst, let him come unto me and drink." (John 7:37)

So how do we apply this to our lives? Speaking to a group on a Wednesday night at University Community Fellowship in Kampala, I asked the question, "How many of you eat three times a day?" Most hands went up. "What about once a day?" Just a few this time. "Twice a week?" No hands. "Once a week?" Again, no hands.

I then asked, "What would happen if you only ate once a week?"

Answers were, "You would get weak, sick, feeble, and eventually you could die."

Spiritually, if we only read scripture on Sundays or Wednesday nights, we would end up the same way as eating once or twice a week. We would get spiritually weak, sick, feeble, and soon would spiritually die. Hunger and thirst are not one-time needs; they are our daily needs. Our bodies need constant nourishment from food and water to function properly. In the same way, our spirit needs daily food too. Many Christians suffer from "spiritual malnourishment" due to lack of hunger and thirst or lack of feeding their spiritual needs. Only God can quench our thirst and satisfy our hunger for His righteousness.

What do you desire most? Do you long for more of God in your life, or have you lost that hunger and thirst?

So, during our prison lesson on Matthew 5:20, with concern the people asked, "How can we enter the kingdom if our righteousness is not greater than that of the Pharisees? They were more scholarly and religious than everyone! They knew the Law and what was required! They were educated, scholarly and worldly. How can it be done?"

Ask yourself if you believe in Jesus Christ as your Lord and Savior. Yes? Then your righteousness is already greater than the Pharisees because righteousness is in Christ Jesus and not us. We must continue that path of truth and not be led astray, because, in this world, there is only one truth and millions of lies.

THE GOOD SAMARITAN

A few months later, as we drove home from the academy, I saw a man lying like a rag doll on the side of the road in the tall grass. I turned around and drove back to check on him to see if he was okay. The way he was lying on the ground worried us; his knee was unnaturally twisted by his forehead. Teacher Emma and I walked up to the nearby house to inquire about him. The lady at the house told us he was a drunk and fell there. The homeowner herself admitted she makes alcohol from fermented bananas, and since the drunk man did not buy it from her, she just decided to leave him there.

We approached him, and I nudged him, and he groaned. I asked Emma what we might do, and we decided to move his leg to a more comfortable position, and we left him there to sleep it off. We got back in the car, and we drove only a few hundred yards when a traffic officer on the side of the road flagged us over. By this time, we were used to getting pulled over for various reasons. Usually for a quick bribe of lunch money was all that was needed, so I started to take out my wallet. He approached us and asked us what was going on up the road where we stopped. I explained the story of the drunk guy, that we'd stopped to see if he was okay, and he was, so we left him there.

The officer said, "Are you sure?"

"Yes" I replied, thinking nothing of it.

He then informed me that down the road a few minutes before we came by someone had pulled over and reported that there was a white man back there standing over a man he had just hit and killed with his car.

I gave a kind of nervous laugh. "No, that's not it at all."

The officer then walked around and looked our car over. There were dents and scrapes all over it from Kampala traffic, of course.

I looked over at Teacher Emma, and his normal smile and happy demeanor had changed to a look of concern, which made me quite nervous because this was now very serious. The prisons are filled with men that are awaiting trial for years based on false accusations and rumors. It was not the first time someone would jump to a conclusion like that, and it certainly would not be the last.

The police officer continued to inspect the car as he walked around. I struggled with the idea of just handing him a larger than normal traffic violation bribe but thought twice because the officer may consider it an admission of guilt and have us arrested right there. After what seemed like a lifetime, he then just nodded his head and let us go. I remembered the time before when Mr. Ssuubi had instructed us to never stop for accidents. I thought about what could have happened, and it could have turned out quite differently. What if he had been dead? I would have been blamed for sure. Would I do it again? Yes. Was I afraid? A little. In summary, I know we should be cautious and avoid dangerous situations, but if I always followed that rule, I would not be living in Uganda, would I?

ANSWERED PRAYERS AND TESTIMONIES

We went to church at the condemned prison and talked on Palm Sunday, and we were able to bring some supplies in to do communion. Through donations we also brought in much-needed guitar strings and picks. There was also an inmate who played the accordion, which was cool. Thanks to all the donations, we had been able to set up a regular schedule to provide the prisons with items such as soap, sugar, toothbrushes, and toothpaste, and most importantly Bibles in a few local languages.

Every Monday morning at the office, we would start the week with worship songs and devotional study of the book of Acts. We had a great day at the Wells of Hope office, doing devotions, completing planning meetings, and financial work. Sometimes we got to do special things, like go to lunch with our friend Pastor Mark, who was just released in Jesus' name from prison after two years. Mark had been waiting for his court date and was released due to lack of evidence. Two years! He made a huge impact preaching and discipling the men while he was confined. Because of prison leaders like Mark and Joshua, the gospel was spreading in the prisons. They may not have always understood why they were there in prison, but they influenced many lives when they did. God's timing is never off.

For Easter, we got to celebrate with some of our family both in the prison and at our house. We had the privilege to visit both the men in Death Row Prison and Murchison Bay Prison. The men in the Death Row Prison were so happy to see us. We were not scheduled to spend this Sunday with them, but we decided to visit them before we went on to the next prison. Both I and inmate Pastor Peter shared the good news that He is ALIVE!! Christ is risen and alive today! No one else can claim that!

Afterwards we joined the men at Murchison Bay Prison. The first two hours were all worship music and testimonies. There was an inmate a few weeks earlier that had a deformed foot and could not put all his weight on it. But that day, he stood before us healed and standing upright on both feet. He said he was no longer disabled, but now able. Two weeks later, we found out he had been released from prison. This is a miracle in itself since he was in prison for such a short time but was changed forever. We continue to pray for Pastor Joshua who would be going to court again for a sentencing.

Pastor Joshua went to court the previous week after two years of waiting, only to find out that the lawyer did not show up. He was told to wait seven more days and come back. Sure, what was seven more days. When he returned, he was told he would have to serve three years. With the time served, he only had ten months left. Praise be to God!

At Boma Prison, we had scheduled the first ever baptism service in the prison's history. The baptisms went very well, and the men at upper prison had an awesome program set up with teaching, reading Scripture, and singing and dancing. All this was thanks to Pastor Sunday, one of our Well of Hope volunteers, who set this all up and brought the pool. But it also had its challenges.

Just about a week before, the prison water main broke and water was in short supply for over 3,000 men. So, over the next seven days, in a place where water is already scarce, men rationed their personal water supply and had to fill at least seventy-five jerry cans full of water to fill the pool. Thanks to the men for the tremendous teamwork, sacrifice, and can-do attitudes. The men from Condemned were also able to come over and share in the event. When it was all over, 150 men were baptized.

We had to leave early and pick-up staff for our weekly hour-and-half drive to the academy. There we had Bible time and a quiz game with Aunt Gina and a game of egg relay with Uncle Steve. Afterwards we celebrated the birthdays as we did on the last Sunday of the month. Most of the children did not know their birthdays, so we just divided them by the twelve months and had fun, singing songs and playing games on their designated day.

This birthday celebration was extra special. We had eight guests visit the academy from a church here in Kampala. After a tour of the academy, the children did a presentation of songs and dancing for the visitors. The guests brought the children gifts of books, school supplies, salt, sugar, biscuits etc. Gina and I noticed there were two goats tied up by the front gate. I commented on the new purchase of the goats we had made, "They will grow fast around here."

The farm hand Julius gave me a strange look, and minutes later brought a goat over by the building and killed it right there, Gina was not happy about that. I stood there holding hands with the smallest boys and watched as Julius showed the older boys how to slaughter a goat and prepare it for cooking. It was all a part of life; there was no supermarket out there.

The visitors ended the day with a football game between the children and visitors. And something happened that made the visit even more special. The Sunday prior, at Boma Prison's worship service, an inmate came to me with a book he had written that consisted of about 175 to 200 handwritten pages of his life. He asked me to explore options and maybe see if I could get it published. I was in shock and told him I have no idea what to do with it, but I nodded my head and took the stack of pages with me. I learned to just trust in God and believe He was doing something I may not understand. The next day at the academy, as those visitors introduced themselves to the children, one young lady said she was a book editor and publisher in Kampala. I simply walked up to her and handed the book over to her. When you are not sure what to do, trust in God, nod your head, and walk in faith.

A while later, Mr. Ssuubi, Gina, and I had returned from our tracing trip to the northeast corner of Uganda. We were gone for four days and traced fourteen families and located and documented fifty-four children of prisoners. The area we traveled to was one of the most underdeveloped areas in the country. Clothes were still optional, and there was no power to be found. The area was called Kitido, and the people are the Karamajong, which in translation means, "old man got tired, stopped and sat down." They are cattle people and warriors to this day. The roads to this area were more like dry riverbeds, and you could drive for six hours and never see another car or person. When you think of remote Africa, this is it.

We left Mbale, and after we had driven for about two hours into the open terrain, I asked the director, Mr. Ssuubi, how far he thought it was to the next petrol station. He replied that he had no idea because this was the farthest, he had ever been from Kampala in his life.

Many gave us advice about the area, but as we traveled, we learned many Ugandans had never ventured into this area of the country, they had only heard about it. We loved it there and were planning a return trip there on our own or with some friends to go camping.

When we returned to Kampala, we sat down with each inmate and presented them with pictures of their children or grandchildren that they could keep. We gave them a full report of how their family was. If the child received a sponsor, they could be brought to the academy for schooling.

When we approached a family while tracing, we asked them "Are you the family of Peter Odong?" to which they replied, "Yes."

"We are from Wells of Hope, and Peter sent us to check on you and his children." They were so shocked. Some of the families never even knew the inmate was alive after years of being missing. It was awesome to get to see the smiles on their faces, hearing their relative was alive.

We would take a photo of the family, and often village friends would join in. We would then print out the photo and bring it to the inmate to keep. The inmate would then sit down and tell us stories of family members in the picture or a memory of a friend that he grew up with who is now caring for the inmate's family. It was a blessing to see the difference a photo could make in the lives of inmates. Many of the men started to attend the Bible study at the prison because of the ministry. Visiting the parents, families, and friends was what we loved to do, almost as much as visiting the children. We even wished we lived closer to the academy so we could visit the children more often, but we lived ninety minutes away, and getting there twice a week was already a lot.

TENSE CULTURAL NEGOTIATIONS

Gina, I, and Marjorie, the assistant director of Well of Hope, drove to Kayunga Uganda, about three and a half hours north to check on two students, Hope and Bernard, who did not return from school break with their families. Their mother had refused to send them back to the school after break for reasons unknown. We pled with the mother, along with the children's grandfather and mother-in-law, who had been supporting her. All of us urged the mother to let the children return to the school. A crowd started to form around her house, and some villagers also joined in, asking her why she would not take this opportunity to better the life of her children. This was a serious cultural situation we had gotten ourselves into. The last thing we wanted was to cause a problem, publicly shaming her into something that would result in her being shunned by her own people in the village.

When people were shunned, they were cut off from the group. This is hard to understand from the western mentality. In most countries like Africa, Asia, and South America, they do not praise individuality, it is all about what is better for the group. Out there, community means survival.

So, to diffuse the situation we thanked her for her time and told her we respected her decision, and left, turning it over to God. When we were about an hour away, the mother phoned us and said to come get them. We turned around and got the children. Due to the late night, the children stayed with Gina and me at our house. They watched "How to Train Your Dragon" and both seemed to sleep and eat very well. Gina got to play mom, getting a basin of water and wash cloth ready to wash up and showing them how to use the toilet by not standing or squatting on it.

After breakfast, I went to do the dishes, and when I returned, Bernard was reading Yahoo news headlines on my computer. They sure did learn fast. The same day, we learned that we had a sponsor looking for a child, and Bernard now had a sponsor along with his sister Hope.

The following week, we were contacted by a representative of Christian Financial expert, National Radio host, and Best-Selling author, Dave Ramsey. She asked for our Financial Peace University (FPU) success story and how it changed our lives. Gina and I were interviewed by a representative from FPU online. We were able to share with her how the FPU program helped us get organized and pay off $40,000 in debt. We also shared with her how he played a major part in Gina and me sharing the Gospel in Africa. Our story was chosen and posted on his web page, which was encouraging and a big part of our testimony.

The next week, we took a trip out to Masaka to visit four families of prisoners. Not in all the cases, but oftentimes we found that when the fathers were taken to prison for various crimes, the mothers would get remarried and leave the children behind with a family member such as a grandmother. On this trip, we saw one family situation that stood out from the rest. This situation taught me how a split-second decision can rewrite a family's history forever.

That day the grandmother sat Gina and me down and shared with us the story of the night their lives were changed forever. Her youngest daughter had gone to see a friend in the trading center a few miles away, and as she walked home, she was sexually assaulted by a man in the village. After hearing about what had happened, the grandfather (the girl's father) and her two brothers went to confront the man, and, in a fit of rage, clubbed him over the head and killed him. In a second, it was all over, and all three went to prison for murder. The grandmother had lost her husband and both of her sons. She also assumed the position as the head of the family and the responsibility of looking after the two sons' wives and her nine grandchildren.

You could see the love she had for her grandchildren on her face, but you could also see the situation was starting to take a toll on her. Wells of Hope came to visit her that day, and just hearing a personal message that the men in her family were surviving added a spark to her otherwise overwhelmed life.

When we returned to the prison on the next visit, we sat down with all three of the men at the same time to tell them all that we had seen and heard. They were so excited to hear about the family and see pictures we had taken of them and the village area.

When you are in prison, your life outside begins to feel like a dream. Some inmates will forget their children's names and birthdates. Some would even change their own names. I believe deep down inside that they do this as some sort of self-preserving action. It is not something you want to do, but when time goes by so fast, no one can visit, and hope begins to fade away, they feel like they must change something. That day, those men were able to be brought back to reality. They were able to connect the ever-spreading gaps of time in their minds and hold on to something that was not a dream but very real, which was a family that had not forgotten them. Most importantly, they were able to hear about a God who had never left them and loved them very much.

WHOM SHALL I FEAR?

When we got home late, we started dinner at 9:00PM. We had been living and cooking dinner with no power for two days, we were down to our last three candles. Luckily, we cooked with gas... but guess what just ran out?

We were told that the power was out again because someone had stolen the village's transformer for the second time. The time before that, they drained the oil out of the transformer so in burned up. We had been told that they sometimes used the transformer oil to cook with because the shelf life was up to six months of use. So, we had to be aware of fried street food that had an unusual shine to it. There was a good chance it was cooked in transformer oil. Another reason they did it was to keep the people in the surrounding houses in the dark while they looked for an opportunity to break in. There was a couple from Europe that lived next door, and they had break-in attempts often. They had security lights, razor wire, electric wiring, and a guard at night and still had problems. We had our dog Molly and turned all the lights off—not a sound. Having a dog was awesome.

In the morning, we conducted our normal weekly Bible study at the academy. It was good to see the children's faces; it felt like we had not been there for a long time. We shared the story of King Saul wanting to kill David because he was more powerful than Saul was since God was with him. After the Bible study, we gathered all the children who had parents still in prison and had them each write/draw a letter for their parent. The children seemed to really enjoy it. We looked forward to delivering the letters to the parents. We encouraged each child to communicate with their parent through letter writing, which could have counseling value, be very therapeutic, and build relationships for future reunion. While Gina oversaw the letter writing, I met with the non-teaching staff at the academy to go over the rules at the school. It was always good to have meetings with our staff and open the communication door. We got to meet the new head teacher who would be starting the next week. We also met the guard dog for the school. The dog and the cows we had recently purchased were building a great friendship. There were a lot of good changes going on which we were very excited about.

After three days in the dark at our home, our power came on for about ten hours on Wednesday. Then it went back off for an estimated five to six days. We had been calling the power company daily for updates and getting nowhere. Finally, at midnight that night while in bed, I got a call from a repairman who was looking for us. Why would the power company tell me there would be no repairs tonight, but someone showed up at midnight to "fix" the problem? I figured this guy would either fix the power or try to rob me once I came out of the gate. No power for days? Or get robbed? It was worth the risk.

Because it was dark outside, my Ugandan friend David and I walked with our flashlight to the top of the gravel hill to the main road to find the repairman. I chose to carry a Panga, also known as a machete, because private gun ownership was discouraged and very expensive. I carried it with me when I moved around at night for safety reasons. Plus, no one had any doubts that if a white guy walked down the street at night with a machete in his hand, he would use it.

We found a guy at the top of the hill who said he could fix the power. David, the repairman, and

I followed the power lines through maize (corn) fields and behind people's homes of barking dogs to a power pole in the middle of a corn field. It was so dark outside—it was Africa dark. All I could see was David's two feet in front of me as I walked. The dogs barking around us would sometimes come rushing up to our feet, barking, then running away. I admitted to David that I now feared dogs too. He just laughed.

We got to the power pole, which the repairman climbed with his bare feet and rigged a piece of wire from one power source to another, bypassing a breaker to give us power. After a few sparks, the power came on. He did this all in the pitch dark with just me on the ground shining a small flashlight on him. I paid him $5.00 for the service call. It amazed me that someone wasn't dead.

Well, the power was short lived because it went out the next day, and we were told they needed a transformer that had to be brought from South Africa. It would be around a five-days wait.

The next day, we were in Upper Prison Condemned, death row section, for Sunday service. Marjorie, Mr. Ssuubi, Gina, and I spoke to the men in Condemned. I was the main preacher, and the sermon was about making choices. I shared from Matthew 19: 16-30 (the rich young ruler). We had a special time of prayer over the prison and the prison walls. We prayed that each man would receive clear guidance from God and be released in His time. We committed ourselves as believers that we need to pray to God to reduce the number of men behind these walls. That through His grace, the men could leave those walls and preach to the men outside the walls to prevent them from going to prison. They committed to do this until the prison closed its gates forever. It was our prayer that those gates be closed forever, and it had to start with us.

MATTHEW 7:13-14

Enter through the narrow gate. For wide is the gate and broad is the road that leads to destruction, and many enter through it. But small is the gate and narrow the road that leads to life, and only a few find it.

I used a great example that I believe really helped the prisoners understand why the gate and road was so wide. The wide road was where everyone from Kampala traveled to get to the capital city—it was busy, distracting, and dangerous. When a person herded cattle and took them off the wide main road to graze, he would lead them single file into the mountains. Most times, that path was so narrow that you could look at the mountain from the main highway and would never know it was there, but that narrow path would take them to the fertile high ground where they would be safe and fed. You saw the cattle and shepherds in the fertile hills grazing so you knew it was available. You wanted to be out there too but did not know how. No one was able to see the narrow path on their own, so they continued to follow the normal crowd of people.

The Good Shepherd shows us how to find the narrow path with a free map, the Bible. The Word of God shows us how to find the path, to navigate it, and stay on it throughout our entire lives. One of the top reasons most people walk on the wide path is because they are being led astray by false teachers, false prophets, and witch doctors.

Jesus warns us about them in the very next verses after the narrow and wide path lesson, for good reason. The only way to know the difference between who is a false teacher or prophet is to study our Bible and KNOW the truth.

A prisoner brought up a good point that we need to know the difference in signs and wonders and the people that perform them. Especially the verses pertaining to Matthew and Mark.

MATTHEW 7:22

"Many will say to me on that day, Lord, Lord, did we not prophesy in your name, and drive out demons in your name and perform many miracles?"

MARK 16:17

"And these signs will accompany those who believe: in my name they will drive out demons; they will speak in new tongues."

In Matthew, the men he speaks of do the same things, but one thing is different, and that is believing. The first were doing it in His name but did it for their own worldly gain. These were workers of iniquity and evildoers.

The prisoners had so many good questions and knew a lot about the Bible already. We had been teaching them how to really study and understand each verse. It was important, if the verse didn't make complete sense, to go back and read a few verses before it to really understand what God was showing us. "To understand a verse, you must often go in re-verse." Their faith was increasing as God was doing many miracles in the prisons and through the prisoners. They said they were strengthened and encouraged each time we were there; glory be to God.

As we completed our study and walked through Condemned Prison common area, I noticed something different. I noticed that one of the doorways to one of the sections on death row was covered by fresh bricks and mortar. The inmates told me that they no longer needed those cells due to the high number of men being released from death row, so they closed it off. Praise God! The prison was beginning to get smaller!

Lord, Thank you for your Word. I pray for strength and wisdom as we walk in spirit and in truth. Help us to dive deep into your word and give us ears to hear. Give us knowledge to know the difference between the truth and lies. Give us hearts to minister that truth to others.

Chapter 11

THE BEGINNING OR THE END?

Life is all about growth, not our trophies.
— Bear Grylls

AFTER A LONG YEAR, our first visitors were arriving in Uganda! We were very excited to have Gina's parents, Bob and Barb, come to stay for three weeks. They would get to see everything that we do with Wells of Hope, the prison ministry, the school, and tracing the missing children. We prayed that we would be given permission to take them with us into the prison. Also we prayed that we would have a great time together and that God would protect us everywhere we went.

Her parents arrived safely, and we spent a few days at the academy doing Bible studies with the children. Barb and Gina got to make some of the children bracelets from string while Bob and I did repairs on the property and put up new barbwire fencing around the compound. The fencing would keep the cattle and other animals off the property. The main area we wanted to keep clear was the football pitch (soccer field) to prevent the children from having to dodge cow poop while playing soccer. We were able to build three wooden bridges over the water trench to give the children easy access to the play field on the other side. During the rainy season the trenches would overflow, and the property would become a swamp.

Gina's parents went with us to the women's prison to conduct our discipleship program. They had a short visit due to the rain because the chance of escape was much higher on the rainy days. Nobody liked to stand in the rain, so the guards were not as vigilant, and escape was more likely. But as we waited out the storm, they had a chance to talk to a few of the women one on one, and I believe they learned a lot.

Bob and Barb brought two suitcases of children's clothes with them from donors in the States. We also received a generous donation of clothes from the Woolworths clothes store in Kampala. All the children at the academy got new clothes to wear, and the Wells of Hope staff spent a few hours sizing the children.

From Thursday the 28th to Friday the 29th of August 2014, Wells of Hope, in partnership with Bible Society of Uganda, conducted a FACE (Family and Community Engagement) workshop at the Bible House—Bible Society of Uganda Office premises. The workshop/training was aimed at helping wives of prisoners and their children to protect themselves from acquiring HIV/AIDS. I was one of the guest speakers in the morning and discussed how we never go through things alone and how God is always with us and will not forsake us. This was a powerful message to those dealing with the challenges of HIV and having a loved one in prison. This was also a good reminder to myself that we are never alone, especially on the mission field.

(Photo taken by Bob Deboer)

After I spoke at FACE, I was approached by a reporter from Kampala News Radio, and he asked if he could interview me for his radio show.

We went outside, and he turned on a cassette recorder.

"We are here tonight speaking with Pastor Stephen Gant from Wells of Hope..." and he started asking questions.

He caught me off guard, but I managed to not make a fool of myself. He informed me of the times for broadcasting and thanked me. I never listened to it because I didn't like the sound of my own voice.

On our way to the airport to drop off Gina's parents, we stopped by the men's prison to drop off some Bibles and let Gina's parents meet some of the men we ministered to. Since their original permission was denied inside the main prison, we chose to go visit on a normal prison visitation day, expecting just a few prisoners to come out and visit us in the lobby. What we got was not expected at all.

As soon as we got to the front gate no questions were asked, all the guards greeted us warmly, we shook hands with everyone, and they asked if we wanted to come in. It was the right guards at the right time. Gina's parents could go inside, meet some of the men we worked with, and share some stories with them. In Boma, they met some of the Pastors and staff in the prison we minster to. We were able to sit down and talk with a lot of them one on one, and after doing our Bible study in the condemned section, they informed us that some of the men will be going to court tomorrow. We prayed those men would be released!

Every time we visited the prisons, we passed around a prayer request book. That morning I took some time to look through the prayer requests we'd written on Tuesday when we visited two different prisons. It was awesome to see how these men's hearts were changing! The prayer requests used to be mostly about being released from prison and for forgiveness for their crimes. We could now read about how God was working in these men.

The prisoners started asking for spiritual wisdom for themselves and for their families to get saved. They were also looking for strength to preach the gospel both inside and outside the prison. The men no longer thought only of themselves but of others as well. We could see amazing things God was doing within the prisons and with the men and women's hearts. After a very fruitful visit, which included sharing encouragement for the men and us, we dropped off Bibles and took Bob and Barb to the airport to fly back to the States.

Over the last three months, prior to Bob and Barb's visit, we had been asking God to provide us with guidance to make plans and to make everything very clear for us. We received our answer, but it was not what we expected at all.

Gina and I had come to Uganda to serve God in whatever field He wanted us. Now that may sound easy, but it was far from it. After the first year, we realized we were working like the two-week, short-term missionaries. Two-week missionaries have a limited time in the country, so their entire fourteen-day schedule is completely booked. They work for two weeks solid and then fly home, usually exhausted but filled with what God is doing overseas. We were working at a pace that was hard enough to keep up with for two weeks, much less two years, and after a year, we were starting to show signs of wearing down both physically and mentally. In that first year I had learned so much about the hearts of men, it started to affect me personally and physically. It is impossible to get down in the mental mud and not take dirt with you.

We were doing our best to get involved with the day-to-day operations of a Ugandan-run ministry but because of cultural differences, were met with a lot of resistance from our own people. It was hard to understand how Africans spend money and conduct their business. We had been attempting to show them a better way, a way that would take the money much further than they were using it for. We had been focusing on stewardship and a better way that established more accountability.

Gina had a BA in Finance from the University of Wisconsin (Steven's Point) and found out the hard way that, although we had a process and training on finances that could help them manage their money considerably better, it was not going to be that easy. To ask someone to show you their books and receipts in America to help them find a better way could be considered helpful, but in African culture, it could be considered rude and very disrespectful. For a year, we waged the financial war, thinking we were helping, but instead we were slowly isolating ourselves.

After a very frustrating year, we told ourselves that we needed to back off from the finances and budgeting. God seemed to be closing that door and we were still knocking on it with our heads. Work then started to slow down, and all we were really doing was the prison ministry, visiting families, and tracing children, which was still a busy schedule and fine to us. After all, we had been seeing miracles—and changes in the men and women at the prison—and showing the love of Jesus to families all over the country. We felt God wanted us to focus on the prisons and everything we were learning there—and we were learning a lot.

We always wanted to remain sensitive to the Holy Spirit, and we saw prison discipleship as the direction He wanted us going in. I had always believed, and still do, that the key to the world is through the hearts of men. One of the main reasons I wanted to be in the prisons was to study and understand the hearts of those men and find a way to reach them. I believed that men on death row in a third-world country would be a great start. When men would understand the role God has called them to, which is leader, husband, father, and protector, all the ills in life would fall into place. People were being saved, but discipleship was seriously lacking.

Armed with a new direction in men's discipleship in Uganda, we met with a church friend, Godwin, for lunch and we shared our plans with him about where we felt God was leading us. We explained to him that we had learned so much about Uganda in the year that we had been there. Godwin agreed that we had seen and done more than most people would do in ten years. We got an inside view into men's hearts in a death row prison and the inner workings, ups and downs of a Ugandan-run ministry. Through the church we attended in Uganda, University Community Fellowship (UCF), we had been receiving training on the cults that plagued the country and realized that discipleship was needed and needed soon. We believed that men's discipleship was the direction in which we would go. We wanted to form a place where men coming out of prison could be mentored and have the Gospel poured into them through a Paul-and-Timothy type of atmosphere. In Uganda, there were thousands of ministries, and almost all of them were services focused on women and children who were often the collateral damage left behind by sinful men. We would create a men's ministry centrally focused on the root cause of a lot of the country's and the world's problems, which is sin. We needed to help these men discover their identity in God.

In society, we had become professionals at being good Samaritans and helping the victims, but who was going back to talk to the robber? Was anyone putting up streetlights on the road that the man was attacked on? Instead of just focusing on the victims, we would focus on the perpetrators: men not being the spiritual leaders of their families and communities.

As we explained our vision, Godwin seemed very excited and wanted to know more. I even had a possible location picked out. We left that meeting, all in agreement that this was something we needed to pray over and needed God's direction for. We would need to be patient and wait on Him, and this was not something to take lightly. We soon received God's clear guidance in the most unusual way.

The very next day at our home, we were informed via a phone call that we had lost our clearance to get into the prison, and just like that, it was over. We were devastated that the door had pretty much been slammed shut. When we ask for God's direction, we do not always like His answer, but the answer was clear. The answer was no. On a positive note, we did get an answer, and that alone was a blessing.

It turns out, the government said it was a security breach when we visited the prison with

Gina's parents and were allowed into the prison with them. Gina and I had clearance, but her parents did not. The prison staff was so comfortable with Gina and me, that they let us pass right through all the security check points as usual. Due to this breach in security, we were devastated that our permission into the prison had been suspended for an undetermined amount of time. The government would be reviewing the prison procedures and retooling the staff on security measures. They simply had become too comfortable with us.

We felt God had provided a clear decision that the prison ministry was over for now. So, we waited patiently as we sought His guidance for a way forward. We went from working seven days a week to two or three days a week. We asked ourselves if all that time had been wasted? What would we do now? We were left waiting and waiting and waiting.

"The Lord gives, and the Lord takes away, blessed be the name of the Lord."

I was also learning that when He "takes away," He does it to give us something even more important; we must be faithful in waiting on Him. We finally began to rest and wait.

Lord, thank you for providing us with direction, even when it comes in the form of disappointment or the closing of a door in life. Your ways are bigger than our ways. Give us the wisdom to understand our place in your plan and the strength to serve others while we patiently wait on your direction.

Chapter 12

THERE IS NOT MUCH TO DO IN THE WAITING ROOM

I am sure that God keeps no one waiting, unless he sees that it is good for him to wait."

—**C. S. Lewis**

I was no stranger to the idea of a waiting room. When I was sick as a child, my mom would take me to the doctor's office for a checkup. Sometimes I would even get out of school for the day. I would think about all the TV I could watch when I got home or just lay around reading Conan comic books and listening to music on my Walkman. What would I do with all my free time today?

When we arrived at the doctor's office, we were quickly seated in this big room with lots of other people. After some time passed, I would wonder, "Who was next? Is there an order here?"

I would swear they were calling people back who'd walked in after us. It was like anarchy reigned.

This was in the days before video games and handheld devices that we shove in our children's hands to keep them entertained. In those days if you said a handheld device, I thought you were talking about my dad's electric shaver. Sitting in the waiting room, I would start to get upset at what seemed like an eternity of waiting and losing valuable goofing-off time. While we waited, it would only take seconds for my mother to start a conversation with a complete stranger. Soon they would be discussing everything from Bundt cakes to peace in the Middle East. When Mom met a stranger, they were not strangers for long. Grocery store, school, baseball game or doctor's office... it didn't matter. They were now friends and may even exchange recipes.

Finally, they would call my name. I would rise to my feet and walk back as if I had been summoned by the Royal Court. I had been chosen! I was sure we would quickly be whisked down the hallway to see the doctor, get a few pills, and be on our way home.

But to my dismay, we would be taken to another room to, you guessed it, sit, and wait. What did a guy have to do to get out of this place, cough up a lung? As we sat, my mom, seeing that I was getting a little restless would say, "Do you want to play a game?"

Sure, there was nothing left to do here but look at the four walls. I could not get out because they put me in a room with a doorknob located about five feet off the ground. She would pull out a small handful of pennies and split them between us, and we'd toss them at the wall one at a time. Whoever could get closest to the wall would win both pennies. We would go until one person had all the pennies and won. I know it was not World of Warcraft or Disney Channel, but it was kind of fun. My mom had taught me that there was always something to do, even while you wait.

I was also no stranger to being in God's waiting room. Sometimes in life, it feels like God has you in a spiritual holding pattern, just sitting on the bench in the game of life or whatever cliché you can use. In Africa, Gina and I were in His waiting room. During this time, the devil tries to make you think you are off course with God and makes you question your own importance in His plan. He will even start to use those around you to make that point.

Since we lost permission to the prison, no one asked us to do anything or even called us. Just like my days in the Navy, they were moving on without us. We had not heard from anyone in weeks, even people back home at our church seemed to trail off. Our next lesson would be patience and longsuffering. I felt like I was a child in time out.

Webster's Dictionary defines patience as "the state of endurance under difficult circumstances, which can mean persevering in the face of delay or provocation without acting on annoyance/anger in a negative way; or exhibiting forbearance when under strain, especially when faced with longer-term difficulties."

Similar is the use of Biblical longsuffering: "Bearing injuries or provocation for a long time; patient; not easily provoked." We had to break down each part of longsuffering. We must bear provocation, which is action or speech that makes someone annoyed or angry, especially deliberately. We must bear this for a long time. How long? Compared to God, time is irrelevant and belongs to Him. And we were now on His infinite clock.

I again started to think back on the waiting room and waiting to be called. As a child or even an adult today, sitting in the waiting room at the doctor's office or even a hospital was torture to me. Long waits, bad coffee, no good TV channels, just the same boring news stories playing on a loop, nothing but time on my hands. Life was like a waiting room. Sometimes we were unsure of our direction, but sure that we would serve while we waited, and we prayed God would show us how soon.

Think about it. When it comes to a hospital waiting room, people do not go there when their lives are good. People wait for news of a friend or a close family member's health. It can be a place of endless questions and worry. A place of sorrow, loss, pain, and often unanswered whys. Much like life, it can be a place where, without a patient heart and deep faith, the devil can attack the minds of those who wait and are made vulnerable.

Almost every hospital has a chapel in it. A place for someone to go to be with God during their time of need. I have seen a few of these places, and they are usually very nice, complete with stained glass. They look very spiritual. Some even provide a staff of chaplains who stand by to help when needed.

The first question for a chaplain is, why are we waiting for them to come to the chapel? We need to be going out to where the people are.

My friend Todd Lemmon decided to further his service to the Lord and went from retired police officer to fully qualified ER nurse. He takes the spiritual battle to the front lines of the health care community. He has come up with clever ways to minister to those in their most desperate hour. When he comes into the room of a new patient, he tells them, "I've been praying for you since before my shift began, so it's nice to meet the beneficiary of those blessings. I will continue to pray for your ultimate outcomes and abundant life." Or

"I am here to assist you in any way possible because your Creator thinks you're worth dying for, so you're certainly worth whatever it takes to ensure good health."

He sets the standard for compassionate service and does it in the most subtle ways. While applying slip-resistant socks to their feet Todd would say, "Jesus would wash your feet, but I'm just going to put socks on them. Still, I work for the same guy. He sent me to take great care of you and I don't intend to disappoint Him."

When people comment about the outward appearance of his cross necklace he would politely respond with "Thank you. I hope the cross on my heart is more evident than the one around my neck." We can all strive to be Christ to someone in a very difficult situation.

Which brings us to the second question we should ask ourselves which is, why are we waiting for the chaplain to go to them? When we that are hurting with them are in the waiting room, we need to pray and encourage those who are in the waiting room with us. There is no need to just wait in the waiting room. Just because we are waiting does not mean we should stop serving. As Christians, we need to assume the spiritual leadership role in these life situations and no longer just sit by and wait. We need to meet people right where they are in the waiting room. We need to pray for them in the waiting room in the hospital and the waiting room of life. We need to go to the sick, not sit and wait for them to come. Use every opportunity you can to ask about prayer requests and concerns. Do not say you will be praying for them but pray with them right then and there. Like my mother showed me, there is always something to do, even while you wait.

After the loss of permission to go to the prisons, we were not sure of our direction, but being patient all the same. We felt and saw the awesome discipleship impact in the prisons on a large scale. We were thankful for all that God had showed us during that season. Now with that door closed, we had more time on our hands. What would we do while we waited? We found ourselves in God's waiting room and decided we would do like John Waller's song says, "I will serve you while I'm waiting."

Teaching Wells of Hope the financial ways of the west became frustrating, and the prison ministry doors had been closed, but we were determined to move forward to other doors and serve Him while we waited.

Colossians 3:17 says, "And whatsoever ye do in word or deed, do all in the name of the LORD Jesus, giving thanks to God and the Father by Him."

We turned our focus to discipleship of the Ugandan staff and volunteers from other churches who would go to the prison in our place, putting the ownership back on the local people, where it should have been in the first place. On Mondays at the Wells of Hope office, we always had devotions to start the week, and we were able to continue our verse-by-verse study of the book of Acts and the early church. The focus was to learn how God uses anyone and everyone for His purpose. Mondays at the office took on a whole new meaning. I would no longer take charge of each session but focus on giving the staff a chance to find their way through each Scripture. Gina continued to plan and coordinate the children's Thursday and Saturday Bible lessons with questions and games. We started to split the children into two groups. Gina took the younger ones for their study, and I took the older ones. This way we could focus on each group and their learning levels, which became much more productive. The older ones worked on memory verses and books of the Bible. It amazed me how the children were able to memorize the books of the Bible and verses which can be a struggle for some adults who already speak English.

We also could survey the property for future building and repair projects. A few Sundays, I was also able to share with the children some more in-depth Scripture reading. I explained some of the parables and what they meant and discussed how we can apply it to our lives today. I was always encouraged by the questions the children asked, which caught me off guard many times.

We were also still attending church on Wednesday nights at UCF in Kampala. We would have a short lesson as a large group, then we would break off into our small groups to discuss it more in depth. Gina and I became leaders in our small group. This time of sharing became very fruitful when we could practice the study of His word with other believers, both to us and them.

We began talking about relationships, feelings, and emotions, which was a major step forward in African culture. Africans did not talk about emotions and feelings. During our small groups, we could answer questions they had and give Scripture references that we had been studying. We never realized how many questions there were or things that were not understood about the Bible. We ended up doing a lot of teaching and study in preparation for all our classes and small groups. You learn more by preparing for a lesson than at any other time just sitting and listening. Take your notes from church home and dig deeper into it during the week. You will be surprised at how much more you understand and learn.

We were also able to travel more with the time we had and could do it cheaper because of our East African visas. In two years, we were finally able to travel and see other countries. We drove and flew to places like Tanzania, Rwanda, and Kenya. We were blessed to be able to see what God had provided for us and to enjoy His creation. Because we had driven ourselves all over the country of Uganda, we were confident to drive ourselves all over East Africa.

The extra time had given us the opportunity to visit one of the places on my bucket list. One of the first out of country drives we did was to drive ourselves and two friends from Kampala, Uganda to Kigali, Rwanda.

RWANDA
(PRONOUNCED RHONDA)

We drove through the winding roads of southwestern Uganda and into the lush green mountains of northern Rwanda. We drove right past the Volcanos National Park made famous for the rare, silver-back gorillas. I relished the opportunity to study and read more about the dark history of this vibrant and colorful country.

As we crossed the southern Ugandan border, the driving went from the left side back to the right side and was a little strange because the steering wheel was still on the right, which made it hard to pass cars. In the capital of Kigali, we were treated to beautiful, paved streets, modern buildings, and the infrastructure of a well-organized, modern city.

Everything was very modern and had a sense of unity about it, but underneath the beautiful exterior of the lush countryside was a deep dark past which unfolded just two decades before, in 1994. April 6th began a hundred-day long genocide that killed an estimated one million people, the majority being Tutsi men, women, and children, mostly with the use of machetes and clubs.

We stayed in a hostel in Kigali, and during this visit, I was able to study firsthand the complete story of what happened as seen throughout the genocide museum and historic sites. We were able to visit the four separate memorials all built on the sights in which it happened. Each one was dedicated to the remembrance of those killed during that dark time.

I struggled to understand what would cause a country that was eighty-five percent Christian to turn on each other just days after celebrating Easter services of our risen Savior. As the people ran, they went to the only place they thought was safe, the church building. There was no refuge there, and most of the people were killed in the same churches they worshiped in just days before with their killers.

There are tragic firsthand stories about this time in Gen Romero Dalliare's book *Shake Hands With the Devil* while he served as a United Nations Liaison in Rwanda. *Mirror to the church* by Emmanuel Katongole also draws attention to the killer's foundational belief that "tribal blood runs deeper than baptismal waters." It was so sad to realize how men would machete and club to death a million people in a hundred days and during that same time still take communion every Sunday.

It was an eye-opening experience and a look inside the darkness of men's hearts and the shallowness of believers. The truth is, in many cases, cultural beliefs override the blood of the cross. You think this is only in Africa? Do you think this was a century ago? Even in our own American culture, some would directly defy the Word of God for the sake of the American Dream. This was not something that we read about in history books from long ago, it happened during my lifetime, which made it even more real. I could've talked to people on the street that very day, and they would have spoken as if it happened yesterday. Some even walked around, pretending it did not even happen in the hopes that it would all just go away.

MOMBASA, KENYA

Another trip Gina and I took was to Mombasa, Kenya. The children's return from school break had been pushed back throughout Uganda for almost a month and a half due to the presidential elections being held Feb 18th, 2016. People were expecting violence to break out if the current president, Yoweri Museveni of thirty years got re-elected for a fifth term. If a coup were to happen, it would be better if the children were separated and at their homes with family in the villages.

Gina and I decided that we would take off by ourselves for two weeks to drive across Kenya. We drove from Kampala to the capital city, Nairobi to Mombasa on the Indian Ocean. We would drive over 1,300 miles round trip and did it backpack style, living out of a carry-on and staying in backpacker hostels all over the country. Most of those rooms were cheaper than a motel in the United States for two people and included some meals, Wi-Fi, and lounging areas and beautiful views. It was definitely the way to travel!

NAIROBI TO MASAI-MARA

While in Nairobi, sometimes referred to as "Ni rob you" due to the high crime levels, we were set up to go on a safari at the Masai-Mara National Park on the southern part of Kenya which bordered Tanzania. The site was famous for the great migration of wildebeests by the tens of thousands crossing over into the Serengeti National Park at the base of Mt. Kilimanjaro. We stayed overnight in Nairobi and had debated whether to drive ourselves south to the Maasai-Mara or hire a company to take us. We decided to hire a company and were glad we did. The day we were set to pay and leave, I started to feel terrible. It felt like Pach-wach in Northern Uganda all over again. I asked the van driver if we could get a refund if I was too sick, and he said, "No." So, I went into the gas station restroom, threw up, prayed, and climbed into the van for the eight-hour ride south.

The choice to have someone drive us was a wise one. When we got south, there was not a single sign directing us to one of the most popular parks in East Africa. Only dirt roads and animal trails leading in all different directions, and not a soul around. Only the occasional stop for a tree in the road and a tribesman standing by to collect a toll for crossing the land area. We would pay some small fee, and they would move the tree for us. When we got to the park, we stayed in a canvas tent, and I had the best night's sleep ever. By the morning my fever had subsided, and I started to feel better. We got to meet a Masai tribe, the son of the Chief and we were accepted as part of the tribe.

After returning to Nairobi, we stayed the night to prepare ourselves for the longest drive, going from Nairobi to Malindi on the Indian Ocean, about two-thirds of the way up the coast towards Somalia, passing through Mombasa. Mombasa is a shipping port and the gateway to East Africa. Pretty much everything that goes to East Africa comes through Mombasa and is then carried down a two-lane road by thousands of trucks going maximum speed towards Nairobi. On a map, it looked straightforward and easy, but, it took us fourteen hours to drive because the roads were so bad, and there were so many trucks. There was not much out there, no hotel or rest area, nothing but trucks, railroad tracks, and zebras.

(Photo taken by the author)
Gina and I being accepted into a Massi Tribe in Southern Kenya

Once we arrived in Mombasa, the sun was going down, and we still had to drive at least two hours north. We stopped at what I believe was a fried chicken restaurant and ordered some food. I tried to call our place to get directions but got no answer. It got dark and we really had no idea where we were going. As we drove north along the costal road, we were stopped at an armed check point by government soldiers. The solider asked where we were heading, and we explained our situation to him. They were not sure of the location but pointed us towards the next main township and warned us about not driving too far north. I am sure there was nothing strange about two white people, lost and driving north towards Somalia. We made it to our place and rested by the Indian Ocean for the next few days. We spent those days between the two cities on the coast, sightseeing and relaxing by the blue waters of the Indian Ocean. We slept in a bedroom built like a tree house, complete with bush babies and monkeys that would visit from time to time at our front door.

The day we were to drive back across to Nairobi, I got sick again. Gina knew what she had to do, and I spent the next eight hours in the passenger's seat in and out of consciousness. At one point, I woke up, and there was an African man sitting in the back seat. Gina explained that she had been stopped by the police and was told to take this man, who she believed to be a policeman, to Nairobi with us. As the saying goes, "Only in Africa."

Although this trip overall seemed to be filled with challenges, near misses, and sick days, we look back on it as one of the best trips we ever took. We love to be challenged and push ourselves to the limit, but nothing pushed us more physically than our trip to Mt. Kilimanjaro, in Tanzania.

MT. KILIMANJARO, TANZANIA
Seeing Mt. Kilimanjaro can be an elusive task. We were staying at the base of the mountain but

were unable to see her for days because of cloud cover. We would walk to the end of the road in the morning and the evening to set up Gina's camera because we were told that it was the best chance to see the peak. After about three days, we finally got a glimpse of the snow-topped peak which could blend into the clouds on an overcast day.

We decided to get an even closer look at the mountain on Gina's birthday. We had met a teenaged couple from Australia days before in our hostel. They were there to climb to the top of the mountain in a guided tour. They said it would take three days to hike to the summit with the right gear and two and a half days to come down. They told us about a day hike that goes to the first camp, about a third of the way up and back again in the same day. A day hike sounded like fun and something we might enjoy. We had been walking all over the city the day before and seeing some of the sights on foot. We'd checked out a waterfall, a market, and an underground village where villagers would hide out during cattle raids by other tribes. So, a day hike one third of the way up Kilimanjaro couldn't be that bad. The plan was that the day of Gina's birthday, we would catch a ride up to the Kilimanjaro Park entrance and go from there.

After paying the fee to hike, they gave us a guide to take us on the day hike. We didn't know what to expect, and our guide was a Tanzanian gentleman of about sixty years old, wearing his Sunday clothes and dress shoes. By the sight of the man, I figured it would literally be a walk in the park.

He then asked us where our rain gear and hiking sticks were. We informed him that we did not have any, so he took us to the rental office to get the gear. Gina and I were not dressed for the weather conditions of the mountain range at all. He further explained that the weather could change in minutes, and it could rain at any time and drop several degrees without notice. We were told that the average time was three hours up, and we would break for lunch at the first camp, the Mandara Huts. Then, after lunch, it would take two hours to get down to the front gate of the park.

We headed off on our adventure and were excited about what we were about to do. The climb began relatively easy, but over the next half hour, it started to get steep. Gina was faced with her old nemeses, roots and rocks. Historically Gina has always struggled with rugged terrain, and this one was a formidable foe. After a while, we saw a sign that read Mandara Huts: 8 kilometers. I started to do the math in my head and realized that this was no leisurely trail walk. This was going to be five miles of uphill terrain for the next three hours.

We counted the kilometers as they passed by and made it sort of a game. We would tell ourselves, "Just make it to the next one, then the next." It was a beautiful, wooded landscape all around us, and the only thing that blocked the view of the sky was the thick green canopy of trees that were over our heads, giving us shade. This same shade would begin to get cooler and cooler as we got higher in elevation. Below our feet was something else entirely. We were crossing miles of roots and rocks that went on like a stair-stepper machine that you wanted to unplug. After four hours, we finally made it to the Mandara Huts. We had climbed five miles in distance and went from 4,500 feet of elevation to 9,100 feet at a forty-five-degree angle.

We sat down for lunch at the huts and were treated to a view of a valley below. We were so high up the mountain, we were above the cloud line, and the temperature had dropped fifteen degrees. We were inside the very clouds that just days before had obscured our view of the mountain from the ground. We had made it a third of the way up the mountain, and we could no longer feel our legs.

We had twenty minutes to eat the lunch, then we had to pack and head down. Because of the extra hour it took, we needed to leave sooner. It dawned on us that we had made it up but would now have to do the same distance going down. As we began to leave the camp, Gina slipped on some loose gravel and lost her footing. The guide asked her to go ahead, and he grabbed my arm and asked me, "Is she going to make it?"

Gina sometimes slipped on level pavement so I believed she would be fine. He explained to me that there was a road that came to this camp in an emergency. It could take people down, but once we passed that road a few feet ahead of us, there was no other way a vehicle could reach us. I thought about it for a second and told him Gina would be fine. In her defense, she doesn't look like it, but she is one tough chick.

Downhill for me was easier because I could jog down, but Gina did not want to lose her footing and get hurt. I held her hand sometimes and would help her along as a loving husband, then the guide would take her hand and seemed to be almost dragging her. I am sure this was not the birthday that she had planned at all. The guide knew we were behind schedule, and we needed to get to the front gate before it closed for the night. I could see the urgency in his face.

On the way down, men were passing us going up the mountain. These were local men that were carrying fifty-plus pounds of supplies on their heads. They were leading groups of climbers who were going to the top over the next week. It gave me my second wind seeing others heading up. I felt like we had accomplished something significant. We even passed by the couple from Australia on their way up to the top. The look of shock on their faces was funny to see. I even joked with them that we had just come from the peak, and the view was worth it.

I asked our guide how he was able to climb with such ease in his Sunday shoes. He replied, "I have climbed to the top of Kilimanjaro over a hundred times in my lifetime as a guide, just like those young men you just saw." Well, that explained a lot. When it was all over, Gina and I had accomplished something that not many people could say they have done. We hiked over ten miles of Mt. Kilimanjaro to above the clouds to an elevation of 9,100 feet above sea level.

(Photo taken by the Author)
Gina and I making it to our destination, a third of the way up Mt. Kilimanjaro.

Learning about history, getting out of our comfort zone, pushing ourselves to the limit was what we needed to do. One of the most powerful things was bonding with my spouse to make a more powerful ministry team for the Lord. When the next time God asks you to do something, trust your life experiences have prepared you for the next chapter of service. You must open yourselves to them and go for it.

In the waiting room, we were not only pushing ourselves with travel challenges, but also learning and teaching. I even had enough time to write seventy-five percent of this book you are reading now, something I never would have been able to do if I did not have the time provided. Gina began to take more and more pictures for use at Wells of Hope. She was able to practice the photography that she loves and serve someone else at the same time. She also set a goal to not only read the Bible in a year, but to better understand it. I am very proud of her, and her knowledge in the Word has grown a hundredfold.

We were able to take some training courses on children's ministry through "Kids at Heart" and another course called, "When Helping Hurts," based on the book by Brian Fikkert and Steve Corbett. We learned more about what poverty really is and how we sometimes mean well but end up doing more damage than good to those we mean to help.

The book, *When Helping Hurts* is a must read for anyone looking to enter the ministry field, to better understand our role as servants of God and the people we serve. In fact, it is a must read for anyone interested in helping others. It gives perspectives on better understanding the key principle of brokenness and that true poverty is not based on money or economic status. Both the rich and poor suffer from this poverty, it is why the rich still feel empty and wanting even though they have money. It is what keeps both the materially rich and poor from living a fruitful purpose-filled life for the Lord.

True poverty is not just lack of food, clothes, and shelter. But when you really get down to it, it's about hopelessness, depression, shame, lack of voice, social isolation, and fatalism. Like a doctor, if we misdiagnose the problem, we never really help the person.

For example, lack of food, shelter, and clothing is the pain that we see. By providing these things, it is like giving them an aspirin when really, they have a broken arm. Social isolation, depression, hopelessness etc. is the broken bone. True poverty is four things 1) the lack of spiritual intimacy with God, 2) the lack of understanding of who they are in God, 3) not being part of a community with believers, 4) lacking the stewardship of God's gifts and material items. [3]

PSALMS 30:8-9

---

[3] Steve Corbett, Brian Fikkert. "When Helping Hurts" pg. 128.

> ⁸ *Remove far from me vanity*
> *and lies: give me neither poverty*
> *nor riches; feed me with food*
> *convenient for me:*
>
> > ⁹ *Lest I be full, and deny*
> > *thee, and say, Who is the* LORD?
> > *or lest I be poor, and steal, and*
> > *take the name of my God in*
> > *vain.*

We must understand that true poverty knows no social or economic boundaries. Teaching this concept and class twice in Africa has already brought about change in those around us. Glory be to God.

What I'd like to pass on to everyone is this. Every person is part of God's master plan. From my experience, we are here to do two things. Firstly, to worship God in spirit and truth through word, song, and action. Secondly, to introduce the reconciliation process between men and the God that created them. This is all made possible through His Son Jesus Christ. You and I are created in God's image, and because of sin, we fell from His grace. But through faith in the shed blood of Jesus on the cross and His resurrection from the dead, we can be reconciled to God.

If you trace back the roots of every sinful act in the world, they would all be cancelled out if each one of us had true spiritual intimacy with God. Could you imagine a life without greed, murder, corruption? Every man, woman, and child worshiping God in unity, free from agendas? I can imagine that; it is called the Kingdom of Heaven.

This life we seek was and still is God's original plan from the beginning. It all began at the tree of life in the first book of the Bible, Genesis, chapter 2. Then, in the new reconciled world in the last book of the Bible, Revelation chapter 22, once again it goes back to, you guessed it, the tree of life.

We are commanded to prepare the people for the kingdom of God. Like good soldiers, we need discipline and training. While you are waiting, ask and allow the Holy Spirit to show you things you have never seen. Read the Word, participate in small groups, and train yourself. While you are waiting, take online courses or courses at your church. If your church does not teach courses yet, ask your pastor if you can start one. An example could be starting a "Financial Peace University" class to help believers to tithe more by breaking free of being slaves to debt. Start a book club, pick a book like *When Helping Hurts,* and meet weekly to discuss the topics and share learning. Watch a documentary on a topic and discuss it in a group. Start a married couple's class and mentor newlyweds. Always be willing to learn and available to teach. Help your pastor and the staff at your church. Volunteer and do it with a cheerful heart. Nothing you learn for the Lord will be wasted time.

So many come to church to be fed at a spiritual buffet, and that is okay for some, but, depending on your spiritual walk, maybe you are ready to start serving at the head of the line. You are ready to move on from the milk to the solid food. Start or participate in a discipleship program and follow through with it. Get to know your spiritual family, and I mean really get to know them. Find a Paul that you can go to for guidance and study the Word of God. The pastor cannot and should not do it all by himself; that is why we are the body, all working in unison.

Instead of waiting around after the prison ministry stopped, Gina and I busied ourselves with study and teaching. What we thought would be something to pass the time now started looking like ministry opportunities all around us. All we had to do was look. Ministry is ministry, big or small, whether it's five hundred in prison or five in a small group. If it's for God, it is never in vain. The key was not to give up or give in.

Look at how you spend your time. So many just think they do not have enough time to do anything. Look at how you spend your time and trim back what is not important to the Lord or His kingdom. We had learned that the things that mean the most require time. Building deep, trust-filled relationships take time. Pushing yourself to the limits and finding fulfillment in your calling is rewarding. But now, seeing the bigger picture, the little worldly things might get us through the day, but the hope in the Lord will get us through life.

During our last month of 2016, I made our two-year-in-review music video, and it can be viewed on YouTube: Gant Missions: Two Years in Uganda.[4] We were able to see the vast impact that had been made by God all around us. We were no longer going to the prisons but were in God's waiting room. The world's waiting room is the perfect grounds for ministry. In the waiting room of life, people are hurt and waiting with minds full of questions. What better time to minister to someone than while we wait for the blessed hope that is Christ's return?

There is a term people use as you are leaving on a journey, "Godspeed." I never fully understood that until we worked in Africa, and we had to have God slow us down. We had to go at His speed so we could learn that an impact can be made large or small in His kingdom. We just had to be willing to serve, and God would provide the opportunity to do it, wherever we were, whether it was to five hundred or five. Eugene Peterson once said, "There is no place on Earth without the potential for unearthing

---

[4] Gant Missions Two Years in Uganda.
https://www.youtube.com/watch?v=KW_mQbGnulA

holiness, right where we are, with these people we are with."

When things get hard and you get into the valley of life, prepare yourself for the climb ahead. All too often, we try to go backwards to the peak we were on before. We try to recreate the successful experience we had in the past and live in it like some magic formula for spirituality. Craig Groeschel said that "we need to enjoy the time in the valley because there are no farms on the mountain top. Growth happens in the valleys."

Start by asking yourself these questions:

1. Are you willing to give up control to serve?

2. Will you be able to remove the distractors that make your life "busy?"

3. List the things that make your life busy. (Put them in order of kingdom importance.)

4. What are you going to do in your world waiting room?

Lord, give us opportunities to creatively serve others in ways we never thought possible. I pray that we no longer sit by in life but meet them right where they are. May we look at our daily lives with fresh eyes and everything we do as an opportunity to serve someone.

Chapter 13

SEASONS AND SEMESTERS

"To everything (turn, turn, turn)
There is a season (turn, turn, turn)
And a time for every purpose, under heaven"
—The Byrds

AS THE BYRDS TAUGHT US in the 60's, every season will bring turns and changes. Change can be a scary thing, but there is a reason for each event. We become creatures of habit, and, depending on our comfort zone, will determine how well we adapt to that change. When Gina and I finished our two-year commitment in Africa, we came home to begin the next season of our life. We knew we would serve the Lord but weren't sure where. Again, it was a major life change, and we were not sure how the transition would go.

We had lived in the African culture for two years and had made many adjustments along the way, and when we got back to the States, reverse culture shock became very real. We learned that culture shock can go both ways. Understanding culture shock sounds easy, but there is much more to it than experiencing a lifestyle different than your own or seeing something you have never experienced before. Here is the easiest way to describe the roots of culture shock.

Your mind has certain checkpoints it meets in everyday life. *I can sit in a chair. I can walk in the store. I can trust the person standing next to me.* Your mind goes through hundreds of these little checkpoints every day without you even realizing it. There are thousands of small things that do not even require you to think about them because they are so normal. I would call them life assumptions. Some examples include stopping at a stop sign, waiting in line, or asking a question without ulterior motives. It is a simple thought process based on your view of the world, your beliefs of right and wrong, and your values in which you assume everyone has a similar base line.

When you first arrive in a new culture, or are only there for a few weeks, things can seem strange and downright awkward, and that is just the things you can see. You laugh it off and tell yourself it is just their way. Very little change will happen inside of you, and you can go home with some good stories about those crazy people you saw. For example, how no one actually ever stops at a stop sign or waits in line, just walks in front of you because what they have to do is more important.

When I was flying out of Addis Ababa, Ethiopia I was about to put my stuff on the security belt at the airport after waiting in line, and an African gentleman walked right in front of me, moved my stuff over, took his shoes off, and put them on the belt. My first reaction was to knock his shoes off the belt and go around him. I was told later by a national that it is okay for people to step in line in front of you, no questions asked. The assumption must be made that they must be important and, in a hurry, to get somewhere, so it is allowed. In the African culture that is normal. Coming from America, this would usually result in a verbal response or physical altercation, but in your new culture, you must adapt to the new normal.

Everything you begin to see and do in your new culture is different. For short trips, you can laugh it off, but when you are immersed in that culture for long periods of time, your brain tries to meet the hundreds of check points of your normal, and the connections are no longer there. You start to feel disoriented and, at times, even hostile.

Upon our return, we were trying not to get caught up in the high-paced life of the United States, but that proved difficult. We applied what Dave Ramsey had taught us about a monthly budget meeting and started to do time budget meetings. Gina and I would sit down and plan out our days to spend our time wisely. We would begin to throw around ideas of what direction we felt God was leading us in, knowing there is always a next step in life.

As mentioned before, ministry on the mission field can be hard. You get the sense of out of sight, out of mind. Although people say they are praying for you, you miss the face-to-face time being home gives you. Our first Sunday back at our home church, we hardly knew anyone. We were greeted at the door with introductions and questions of, "Welcome!! Is this your first time at East Pointe?"

Pastor David Patrick was the new lead pastor at East Pointe, and we had never met him before because Pastor Dave took over after we were already in Africa. Gina and I had not been part of any type of mission's organization, and the support money that was sent usually came from three sources: friends, family, and church members. We did not have a lot of financial support from other churches, which was how most missionaries got funded. Our biggest support came from family and friends. All that support was sent through East Pointe Church to us on the field, which is not the normal way to do things and does not happen too often today.

When we returned home to Jacksonville, we set up two meetings. The first was to fly to Amarillo, TX and debrief Partners in Hope (PIH). PIH is an organization we learned about that helps raise money for Wells of Hope. It was started by Brooke and Gabe Skypala after they took a trip to Wells of Hope in Uganda and felt the need to raise support for that ministry. We had a great time meeting them and sharing all we had seen and what God had done through us in Uganda. Our first meeting at the restaurant in Amarillo was so long, that we went for breakfast and coffee and stayed to order lunch. It was refreshing and therapeutic to just sit and tell them everything. We had a chance to go to their church and share our story and slides with their Sunday School class.

Upon our return to Jacksonville, FL, we sat down in a meeting with Pastor Dave. We showed him our video and shared with him what we had been doing for the Kingdom while in Uganda. He said that he liked the level of enthusiasm we had and that I reminded him of Apollos in the New Testament. Now this statement had a profound effect on me, so much so that I started to study who Apollos really was, I started studying the traits of Apollos and how I fit into his likeness.

Acts 18:24 states that Apollos was a Jew, "a native of Alexandria," which means he grew up in that noted center of the Hellenistic (Greek) world where Gentile and Jewish learning met and interacted. I also had grown up in the religious epicenter, which is the Bible belt of South Carolina where Biblical doctrine and worldliness collided.

Scripture describes Apollos as "an eloquent man, and mighty in the scriptures." Verse 25 says, "This man was instructed in the way of the LORD; and being fervent in the spirit, he spoke and taught diligently the things of the LORD, knowing only the baptism of John." He was doing great things and was on fire for the Lord even though he had a limited understanding of the Word.

Apollos possessed not only a well-stored mind but also a natural facility of speech. He was proficient in teaching and debating. He had also developed the valuable trait of accuracy and a solid method in study and teaching. This was an early example of what we understand today as hermeneutics. In the most basic definition, hermeneutics is a method or theory of interpretation of language, whether written or spoken. Generally, hermeneutics is an activity that interests Biblical scholars, but the Word is sometimes used in philosophy as well. For example, if you enjoy sitting in a library, pouring over the same book for hours from every angle, then you will love hermeneutics.

I did have the trait of speaking and teaching in public because of my many years as a facilitator and instructor in the Navy. Once I was saved, I would take my love for learning and my free gift of salvation and put them together. I immediately went out with the fire and determination of a Chief Petty Officer in the Navy and started to disciple others, and I would continue to train others through my testimony.

Acts 18:26 continues, "And he began to speak boldly in the synagogue: whom when Aquila and Priscilla had heard, they took him unto them, and expounded unto him the way of God more perfectly."

In the audience that day were two lay Christians, Priscilla, and Aquila. They doubtless were impressed with the fervor of Apollos but saw that he was lacking a few details that were important to the ministry. They apparently took Apollos to their home and tactfully "expounded to him the way of God more accurately."

They saw Apollos as God saw him. They saw someone that had a gift and needed to be discipled. This may sound natural, but it is not. They took it beyond just seeing him and acted. When was the last time we saw someone for their gift and helped them use it for the Kingdom? This is the core of discipleship.

As believers, we are at many different levels of spiritual growth and are in desperate need of edification. Romans 14:19 says, "therefore let us pursue the things which make for peace and the things by which one may edify another."

Merriam-Webster's Dictionary defines "edify" as "to instruct or to improve (someone) morally or intellectually." The reason behind edification is to peacefully pursue the things that make each one of us better alongside each other.

Like myself, Apollos had the fire and the drive but was lacking in complete knowledge for "he knew only the baptism of John." This should not be viewed as a negative thing; in fact, it was a positive. Aquila and Priscilla would have looked at him and saw the things he was doing and the passion and power with which he was doing it. They would have seen the raw talent he had and the work that God had inside him, all on a limited big-picture view. They most likely approached him and said something like, "We are impressed with what you are doing and would love to teach you even more. Come to our house, and we will train you in a more perfect way that will take your ministry to the next level." Discipleship is a lifetime event conducted by many people over a lifetime. This would beg the question, how often do we as spiritual leaders reach out to others to know them and disciple them in a better way?

Apollos knew enough to be convinced that Jesus was the Messiah. He "taught accurately the things concerning Jesus," which implies that Apollos did have a general acquaintance with Jesus' ministry and teaching, but he was uninformed concerning the outcome and spiritual results of Christ's mission. Yet even in his limited knowledge concerning Jesus, he was "fervent in spirit," bubbling with enthusiasm and zeal to share it with others. His passion set him on a course to tell others everywhere he could. This kind of flame needs to be fueled and fanned to burn bright through authentic discipleship. From this exchange, I learned that I was seen as enthusiastic and driven but was lacking in something that would bring it all together, like in Apollos's situation, a more perfect way.

Pastor Dave in a sense was pulling me aside and pointing out the fact that I had the fire and the foundational knowledge, but he asked me if I would consider taking it a step further to pull it all together. Yes, I would consider it and no, I was not going to move into his house and learn. But two months later I took a huge step and registered as a freshman and fulltime student at Trinity Baptist College in Jacksonville, FL.

OLD MAN ON CAMPUS

Two schools I considered were Trinity Baptist College (TBC) and Louisiana Baptist University (LBU). Online learning was not really my thing, and Trinity was in Jacksonville, so I planned to attend classes on campus. I was not the oldest on campus but third in line for that title. The two others were also Military Veterans using their GI Bill money.

I had originally signed up for the two-year Biblical studies program until I received a phone call from Dr. John Cash, who introduced himself as the VA representative and registrar for the college. He asked me a few short questions about what I saw myself doing in the future. He then proceeded to explain to me that I would not be signing up for the two-year program but the four-year BA in Pastoral Missions program, "because anything else would be a waste of my time and his." He then changed my degree program over the phone and said he would see me in class.

Being a forty-five-year-old freshman was strange. I had barely made it out of high school alive and had taken a twenty-five-year break from school to earn my Life Degree in the Navy and my PhD in misery from the school of hard knocks.

I showed up for Freshman orientation with loads of real-world experience and felt like a fish out of water. A professor walked down the line of desks introducing himself to students. He introduced himself to a female student next to me and pointed at me. "Is this your father?"

She looked at me with a disgusted look and said, "Um, no!"

I admitted, "No I am not, although I do have daughters older than her. I am Steve Gant and a freshman here at TBC."

The first two years went by like a blur, but I approached school with the same drive, organization, and determination as any Chief Petty Officer would. Working out of my office at home in the beginning proved to be difficult because of all the distractions. It was easy just to walk out of my office and start doing other things around the house. There was Gina, we were also taking in foster kids on a regular basis, and there were chores that needed my attention. Gina and I sat down and made a plan that would help me get through the next three years. I would treat school like a job. Five days a week, I would leave at 8:00 in the morning and go to school until 4:00 and come home. When I got home, there was no homework or projects, just family time. I would go to all my classes during the day and spend the rest of my time studying at school, usually in the library, where I had the same seat in the same corner for the first two years.

It was a fifty-minute drive one way to Trinity Baptist College on the west side of Jacksonville, which was located off Interstate 10. When people asked where TBC is, I would tell them to drive out of Jacksonville on Interstate 10 until you think you are lost, then take the next exit. Most of the drive time every day, I would listen to three things, the audio Bible, audio books for school topics, or Bible podcasts. I had turned my drive into part of my education.

Much like life, half of your learning happens in the classroom, the other half goes on outside of it. I had mastered the classroom learning and study in the library, but starting that third year, I realized that something was off. Halfway through my junior year, I felt that I was missing something, and something had to change. So, I started to ask those I trusted on what I could do about it. The best advice I got came from my classmate Vaughn Brown, who was also seasoned in life like me. We started out in classes together our freshman year and sat together most of the first year and a half. We had both missed out on the real college experience of dorm life, so we decided to call each other "roomie."

Vaughn had assumed the position as Dean of Men at the college and was now referred to as Dean Brown. I got to see him less and less because of the job, but I settled into the idea of calling him Dean Brown and going to him for advice.

He told me that the feeling I was having might be that I put too much focus on the study aspect of school and not enough of the social part. I thought that was a crazy concept at first because most students would throw themselves into the social aspect and for the most part forgo the study, eventually dropping out. He said I needed to get out of the library and mix it up a little bit around campus. I should have known this was true because my closest friend on campus was the librarian, Mrs. Claxton.

I agreed that I would be intentional, and I would start that day. I packed up my books and told Mrs. Claxton my plan and that I would stop by to say hi from time to time. I was moving my operation over to the college coffee shop called HeBrews on the other side of the campus. It was a much more public place with a lot more student traffic. I walked in and set my sights on a corner table and chair, where I would set up camp and continue my work. As I walked to my newly chosen corner, a classmate, Savannah Chandler stopped me and asked me if I would consider the nomination for Chaplain of the Student Body for the next year,

I stared at her blankly and replied, "Sure, why not?"

Within a few days, things were picking up a lot. I made myself available for students to ask me questions about anything, from study habits and homework to relationship advice and employment. I would even occasionally sneak in a sea story from my Navy days. I was there so much that, right before the summer break, I got a job at HeBrews working behind the counter, serving food and coffee. Now I could go to class, study at HeBrews, and walk ten feet to work. I would be able to work and talk to students all while getting paid. The money was never really the point, but guiding young minds was what I loved.

In the four years at Trinity, I never took classes during the summer or Christmas break. That time was for family, and I planned on keeping it that way. Sure, it made the semesters more of a challenge; I was taking seventeen credit hours a semester in addition to being the Student Body Chaplain and now working at HeBrews. I took off for the summer of 2019, knowing the next and final school year would promise to be a good one.

As soon as the summer started, Gina and I had plans to go and spend a week with our entire family in the Dominican Republic for her parents fiftieth anniversary. When we got back to Jacksonville, we had one week to get things together for a five-week stay in Guyana, South America with Greg Mann from Grace Ministries. Greg was the Missions Program professor, and Missions pastor at Trinity Baptist Church, and my mentor. With the help of my friend and classmate Josh Templeton, my plan was to complete my required internship with Greg in Guyana that summer, conducting a teen camp and various visits to the surrounding villages. Upon my return, I would start my senior year.

The flight into Guyana went very well. Travel was smooth, luggage was on time, and the flight into the jungle was scenic. The remoteness of the villages felt good, and everyone was very welcoming. My life up to that point felt like an outlet with too many plugs in it. I was starting to overload, but once I landed in Guyana, the outlet became unplugged.

We would be sleeping in hammocks with mosquito nets and bathing in rivers or using buckets for the next five weeks. We got settled in, and the campers came from different villages. It took most of the first day to register all the kids. Some kids were coming from hours away just to be a part of camp. Some kids even arrived by boat after dark because of a bad boat motor. It had taken them nine hours in the blazing sun and covered by a blue tarp in the pouring rain, but they made it and had smiles on their faces when they got there. I could hardly get some American kids to come across the street for camp, much less nine hours in the rain or the sun.

Each year, the students looked forward to this week of camp. Camp started at sunrise, and the teens were ready to go. They would go all day and end around 10:00PM. One day, all the teens and the ten adult leaders went down to the river for a scheduled swim time. I was standing on the little bridge that was about ten feet off the water. I took my sandals off and decided to cannon ball into the water. When I came up, I looked up at Josh Templeton and Gina on the bridge and told her as calmly as I could, "I think I broke my foot." I lifted my leg out of the water and my foot just flopped over.

There were no cars in the area except for one transport van of which we knew, and it just happened to be in the area. The van was driven by a camp helper, Damien, and he drove like the devil. I was able to get out of the water, and Damien drove as fast as he could to the nearest medical center without killing us. My foot had detached from my ankle but had not broken through the skin. I held my foot as Greg propped me up during the drive. I do not remember any pain at all, but I do remember Damien sharing an encouraging story as we drove that my foot should be fine. He informed me that the same medical clinic we were going to had fixed his arm, and it worked great. He then showed me his elbow that had a lump on it from what looked like a bone that had not set correctly. He was not boosting my confidence at all.

When we got to the village center clinic, they x-rayed my foot and said they thought my fibula had a small fracture and that my foot was out of joint. They had only done one x-ray with my foot on its side, and it appeared to look fine to them. The x-ray guy propped up my foot and was putting a splint on it with an ace bandage to keep it stable. When he turned to get the bandage, my foot just flopped over again to the point that Greg had to hold it in place by my big toe as he wrapped it. Once it was wrapped up, they said to come back in thirty days. We were in and out in thirty minutes and never saw a doctor. The clinic was free, and they had no pain medication or crutches. On our drive back to the jungle we started to plan for our trip home which would prove to be more of a challenge than originally thought.

Due to the remoteness of our region, there were only two options to get back to the capital city of Georgetown, which was the only city that would have the medical technology to handle this type of situation The first option was a twenty-four-hour boat ride, which sounded fun at first, but this cruise would be in an open hull wooden boat with no cover and a small outboard motor. The other choice was to catch a flight from the interior to the capital. There were three downsides to this. The first was that there were only two planes that came in and out of the jungle once a day, pretty much the same time, and left minutes from each other. The second was they only fit twelve people, and the third was that they were booked for the next two days. Luckily, Gina had brought 500mg Ibuprofen with us, and I borderline overdosed on them every three hours. I had to urinate into a two-liter bottle because I could not get down the stairs to the toilet because of the terrain and no crutches.

After two days, the morning came for our flight, and we had arranged for our friend Delon, at the Georgetown airport to put crutches on the first incoming flight. I would get the crutches and use them to assist myself boarding the second flight minutes later. The problem that day was that the second flight came in first and they were getting ready to board. I had to hop across the dirt runway and crawl up the little ladder to board the plane. Our driver Damion looked concerned that we would miss the crutches by only two minutes.

My flight was full of medical patients, one of which was a little girl that looked to be around three years old. It appeared that she had fallen into a fire and sixty percent of her body was covered in burns and bandages. The other was an elderly woman who was large and needed to be laid in the back of the plane due to her injured back. The flight was delayed for a few minutes as she had to go to the restroom, and it was just long enough for us to hear the whirr of the second plane coming in.

As the plane made its approach to the airport, an injured dog hopped down the dirt runway on a bad leg. There was a tense moment as the plane touched down and the dog scampered away at the last second. I got the crutches, and we made it on the flight to Georgetown. After a day-and-a-half hotel stay, we went from Georgetown to Trinidad, then finally to Fort Lauderdale. Friends Bryan and Stefanie Nicholson from Here2There Ministries drove down to Fort Lauderdale to pick us up and turn around to go back to Jacksonville. It took us a total of five days from the injury to get back to Jacksonville.

The next morning, Gina took me to Naval Hospital, NAS Jax Emergency Room to get a second opinion on my ankle. At first, they did not understand why I was coming into the ER with a splint and bandage, but after I told them the story of Guyana, they took me to get X-rays. The ER decided to change out the splint and send me home so I could make an appointment for the next day to see an orthopedic surgeon. As they began to splint it up again, a Navy Captain walked in wearing scrubs and told them to stop what they were doing. He had happened to look at the X-Rays and saw something he did not like. It turns out my foot was worse than we had all thought. They would say that I broke it good, but in a bad way.

I was told by the surgeon that it would have healed on its own in a third-world country, but in the first world you would need surgery. Because of our missionary lifestyle, surgery was recommended to prevent me dislocating it again while in the jungle. The surgery lasted six hours, and I was the recipient of two brackets, thirteen screws, and forty-eight stitches. There I was again, I would spend the next two months lying on my back, either on the couch or in bed with a wedge elevating my foot, listening to God. A full recovery back to walking again would take about seven months. My summer and senior year was not starting out well.

Because I was off pain medications and the break was on my left foot, I was cleared to drive myself to school to start the fall semester as the new Chaplain and my new job at HeBrews. I had received a knee scooter and zoomed around from class to class. All the students were very helpful and assisted me in carrying out my normal tasks. Because I had laid around so much, I got tired easily. I would have to tell the injury story hundreds of times, and as time went on, I would adopt the name "Cannonball."

The second most-asked question behind "What happened?" was "Why do you think it happened?" I thought long and hard about that answer over my recovery time. We all ask why something happens. I have learned that there are two things that can determine why something happens: God redirecting you, or the devil trying to stop you. The wisdom is knowing the difference. But I joked that there is also a third reason and that is natural stupidity. I tried not to overthink it and prayed about it a lot over the next few months. I felt that God wasn't redirecting me, but, like my back injury recovery many years ago, He was giving me time to reflect in Him and learn more about Him through His Word. I would use the time wisely to study, socialize, and prepare for the next step, whatever that step might be. I have learned that if you do not make time for God, do not be surprised when He clears your schedule for you.

Like my recovery, school would continue, and my senior year went by in a blur. I was proud of the fact that I could maintain a 4.0 GPA, graduating Summa Cum Laude, serve as the Chaplain, and was still able to council students while working at the coffee shop.

After about five months, I had completed my physical therapy and was making good progress. I was able to walk much better and I was even able to walk my daughter Ashton down the aisle on her cruise ship wedding that January.

The reality was setting in that after Spring Break, I would only have eight more weeks, and school would all be over. I could finally see the light at the end of the tunnel. We started to make plans for graduation in May; I had ordered my cap and gown and received my graduation pictures. We were making our initial plans for our return to Guyana with Grace Ministries for my internship that summer and were gathering a team from East Pointe Church to join us.

I was on spring break, and life seemed to be going well but it was also getting to busy. Then one day, all the students were told that the school would be extending spring break for another week. Now what student would not like two weeks of spring break? This break would be different because of a little thing called COVID-19. Everything had been placed in a holding pattern because the virus was serious, and the worst part was I would eventually contract it.

After I contracted Covid-19, these were the two most popular questions I got asked. The first was, "How did you get it?" To which I responded with my usual whit and sarcasm told them, "It might have been that time I licked the counter at Lowe's, but I can't be too sure." That usually got a lighthearted chuckle because I seriously did not know. I wore my mask and washed my hands, and I guess I just got sick.

The second question people asked was, "what was it like?" "Well," I would respond, "when you have stared death in the face and come out the other side, it changes a man. You know, the thousand-yard stare." People quickly learn when I get in an awkward situation, I often turn to humor to make the situation lighter.

The truth is I got a low-grade fever and a slight headache after cutting the grass and assumed that I was dehydrated, which is not uncommon in Jacksonville during the summer. For the next five days I drank a lot of water and Gatorade because, besides the fever and headache and feeling drained, not much happened that was cause for concern.

The part that did concern me was I was at my mom and dad's house in Huntersville, NC when I started to feel bad. My sister Robin and brother-in-law were also exposed to me. We also had two boys that had to stay with us from another family from church during that time. Gina was also always by my side, and we were not social distancing. Gina made a stand and never left my side. "If you get it, I get it and we can be sick together." She is the best! Glory be to God that everyone came back negative, and no one had any symptoms, not even Gina.

But what did happen during those weeks of sickness, recovery, and months of isolation, I was able to get more into the Word of God, spend some time kayaking and fishing. Gina and I also finished more books than we had read all the previous year. I was able to write some training programs for Grace Ministries in Guyana and finish this book. Just like life, take the time and opportunities to learn and prayerfully look forward to the direction that God has you on. Good or bad, every experience in life is a learning experience.

(Photo taken from the Author)
August 2020 TBC graduation

Lord, Through the many challenges in life I can now look back and see your hand all over everything. I ask that you continue to guide me in the direction you want me to go, using whatever means necessary to get me there.

Chapter 14

A NEW BEGINNING

*"Nobody can go back and start a new beginning,
But anyone can start today and make a new
ending."*

—Maria Robinson

All too often, we look at other people's lives
and set it as the standard for our own life
development. We look at the highlights of
people's social media page and see it as reality.
We need to stop holding ourselves back by
comparing ourselves to the social media profile of
someone else. Just like the Bible says (Psalm
139:14), each one of us is fearfully and
wonderfully made, and your story and
experience makes you special. God can, and will,
use that if you let Him.

Also, each of our lives has a beginning and
middle that is unique to us. It is our testimony.
Everything we have done and seen, our
beginning and middle, can be used for His
purpose in the here, now, and the future.

One of the key barriers is that we must
recognize and face the patterns of our life. We can
no longer let the negatives of our past control our

future because that is a tool of the devil. When God shows us the truth, and we understand the negative ways our past may be influencing our present, we unlock the power to make different choices, better choices. Our story is not over; in fact, it has just begun.

Another key barrier would be the lack of understanding on how far God will go to get your attention. Often in my life there were serious catastrophic instances and major injuries that resulted in God getting my full and undivided attention. Some will look at that as to extreme. As a result, I tell people this. Never question God's resolve, love, dedication or limits to get your attention and get you back to Him. Especially a God that would sacrifice His own Son to do it.

There is an old African proverb that says, "The best time to plant a tree is twenty-five years ago, the second-best time is now." Set aside time today to reflect on the ups and downs of your own life. Celebrate with God the high points on the mountain and the low points in the valley with equal enthusiasm. Recognize and break down the barriers that go against you and realize that God has been with you the whole time. No time is wasted time. It is all part of God's plan to bring you back to Him, and in turn, use you to get that message out by going and sending.

So, Cori, to make a long story short and to get back to your original question: "What does qualify someone to be a missionary?" All I can tell you is what I know. God made us in His image to worship Him. God is with us and pursues us, no matter how messy our life gets. He desires to bring us back to a place of honor with Him. God puts it on our hearts to serve Him and His people. He gives us His Word, and in that Word a command to fulfill Matthew 28:19 that says, "Go forth and make disciples of all nations and teach them." In a sense, "Go out and bring the people back to me." Gina and I have chosen to answer that call and teach them all He has commanded us.

People ask me about specialized training and schools, which I think are important and have their place in the process. There are phenomenal schools and programs out there that will help you realize your potential, train, and guide you to maximize it, but no special school is needed, just start with direction from God and a willingness to serve. No training or school can give you the willingness to serve others, that comes from your heart. No one can teach you that. Without that willingness to serve, do not bother with a school yet.

First, I would say you need to spend time with the Lord and seek His wisdom. Take some time to prayerfully reflect on all the things you have learned in your life spiritually and socially and allow these experiences to speak to you in the form of a narrative about your future. Take everything you have learned morally, both right and wrong, and learn from them. Often the mistakes we have made can be the most powerful lessons to be learned. Many of us have the scars to prove it. Take inventory of your talents that you have been blessed with by God and combine it all into the calling that God has put on your heart.

Grow in your faith by getting out of your comfort zone. This is vital to your trust in the Lord and your own spiritual growth. You must be willing to go all the way in trusting the Lord. This will even require you to forgo family, friends, and those closest to you. I think about the life of Joseph. He had a vision and calling from God, and when he told his family, it had a negative consequence. Even his own family would betray him, turn on him, and sell him, but it all worked out in accordance with God's perfect plan. In the middle of trials, just like Joseph, we will not always fully understand it, but that is the foundation of faith.

How much are you willing to give up? You need to be willing to give up certain things in life that others may consider normal. In reflection, a lot had to be given up in our journey. We sold most of the extras we owned because we realized that our lives had become full of the day-to-day routine of managing stuff. It also has taken a lot of discipline to manage the money we have with the things we need for the ministry. Not all missionaries will live by the same means. Like with the false perception of social media, be careful not to look at one missionary and try to mold your life to fit theirs because your story is uniquely yours. There are no cookie-cutter answers or life hacks to living a Christ-like life, just be willing to push yourself, and the Lord will grow you from that.

We left behind a lot of the things we enjoyed doing and the people we liked to do them with. The biggest sacrifice we had to make was spending time away from our girls, Ashton, and Gabby.

When the girls were very young, I asked them, "What are you going to remember about your dad the most?"

Their response was, "You sweat a lot!" and "You are a very hard worker!" Not really the kind of eulogy you want recited at your funeral, but it is what it is. After working so hard and so many missed years in the Navy, I was not sure how far I was willing to go. Gina will even tell you there were some tearful nights in Africa, when in the middle of the night, the thought of not having the girls and family around would weigh heavy on our hearts and would cause us to even question why we were even there. These are the things we struggled with in those years in Africa and beyond, but seven years later, my struggle was answered in the form of a postcard written by one of my girls. A postcard which I have hanging on my office wall to this day.

> *Dad,*
> *You have been a great example of how powerful God's grace can be in one's life. I'm so proud to have seen your growth with the Lord. I aspire to have a faith like yours. Thank you for all that you have done. I love you so much!*
> *Love, Gabby*

A short note with a powerful message. I still sweat a lot and am a hard worker, but I'm not doing it for the glory of men, but now am doing it for the right reason. Matthew 5:16, "In the same way, let your light shine before others, so they may see your good works, and glorify your Father in heaven." God is now getting the glory.

Missionary Greg Mann recently passed to me a life lesson and it is this: "When you do things for the Lord, never touch His glory." I want to work hard and sweat for the Lord and give Him the glory. This is what I want to be remembered for and nothing else.

Some people will become missionaries, and some will be supporters, but you must choose one or the other. Some senders may even be sent someday, are you open to go? Both these jobs are equally important in God's Kingdom plan. Both going and sending require a willingness to serve, getting out of your comfort zone and, sacrificing the things of the world that might be holding you back. Remember that God is not sending you away, but you are going to where He is and that is with His people.

In this book I wanted to take a risk and expose the life that I lived. That you would read this and not see the sinner I was, but the clear grace of God that brought me out of it. Then secondly that I believe there are two main phases in the life of the believer. There is the sinner to salvation phase which I pray all of you know or get to know. The second is the one that seems to carry the most struggle which is the salvation to service.

I hope this book plays some small part in helping you in your walk with the Lord and helping you decide whether you are sending or going for the Lord. There is a lot of planning and preparation that goes into both. First and foremost is prayer and to know which one God is calling you to do. Start in your own neighborhood church and work your way to the nations. You do not have to travel the world to make a Kingdom impact. Start today and share with friends and family what you have on your heart and talk to God and your pastor for the next

step. I am praying for you. Call me if you ever
need anything.

Grace and Peace,

Steve Gant

(858) 776-0343

SPECIAL ACKNOWLEDGMENTS

East Pointe Church Jacksonville, Fl
Epcjax.com

Nancy E Wood Editing and Publishing
www.nancyewood.com

Sam Childers at Angels of East Africa
www.machinegunpreacher.org

Francis Ssubbi and the staff at Wells of Hope
Uganda (WHO)
www.wellsofhope.org

Bryan and Stefanie Nicholson Here 2 There Ministries
www.here2there.org

Brook and the team at Partners in hope (PIH)
www.partnersinhopeusa.org

Pastors Micah, Ben, and Patrick and all the staff
at (UCF) University Christian Fellowship in
Kampala, Uganda.
UCF (University Community Fellowship) | Facebook

Mr. Russell Moro in Kampala for your godly
wisdom and legal advice.

Thank you, Wendy Mann at Grace Ministries!

In memory of my friend and bandmate Tom Cook. May 8th, 2019.

ABOUT THE AUTHOR

STEVE GANT has been married to his wife Gina since 2011. They have two daughters, Ashton Smith and Gabrielle Johnson. Steve received his BA in Pastoral Missions from Trinity Baptist College and is a 20 Year Navy Veteran. He is ordained and was the Missions Pastor at East Pointe Church in Jacksonville, Fl. He is currently the Associate Director of Grace Ministries in Guyana, South America. He is an experienced engineer, organizer, and leader that has a passion for seeking out and discipling the lost.

Facebook: Stephen Robert Gant
Email: sgant55@gmail.com
Globalfaithmissions.org

Made in the USA
Columbia, SC
30 November 2021

50077718R00187